CHINESE
MYTHS & LEGENDS

✳ · ✳ · ✳

OBD: To the Carey clan – Fiona, Aoife, Ruth and Maeve
NH: For Lara

The Myths and Legends in this book have been re-told by
O. B. Duane, except *The Crane Maiden and Other Fables* which were written by N. Hutchison.

First published in Great Britain by Brockhampton Press, a member of the Hodder Headline Group,
20 Bloomsbury Street, London WC1B 3QA.

ISBN 1 86019 222 X

A copy of the CIP data is available from the British Library upon request.

Created and produced by Flame Tree Publishing, a part of The Foundry Creative Media Company Limited,
The Long House, Antrobus Road, Chiswick, London W4 5HY.

CHINESE
MYTHS & LEGENDS

O. B. DUANE & N. HUTCHISON

Art Center College of Design
Library
1700 Lida Street
Pasadena, Calif. 91103

CONTENTS

CONTENTS

INTRODUCTION

HINA IS A VAST, SPRAWLING NATION, as geographically diverse as Europe and comparable to the European continent in size, containing at least one third of the world's population. It has always retained a mysterious and captivating appeal, and remains a country of rich contrasts and diverse cultural influences drawn from many different sources over the centuries.

Archaeologists and social historians trace the origin of Chinese civilization back to the twelfth century BC, which is roughly the same date that Greek civilization emerged. Some of the earliest objects uncovered from excavated sites support the existence of a race of simple agriculturalists, known as the Shang, occupying the basin of the Yellow River in the north of the country at about this time. Again, like their Greek counterparts, the Chinese evolved quickly into a sophisticated and efficient people, so that by the fourth century BC, they were able to boast a relatively civilized, structured society.

Unlike other European nations, China was not conquered by foreign invaders, with the result that she remained largely isolated from the West, and was able to preserve her own unique culture and traditions. That is not to say, however, that China remained immune to outside influences or that she was unduly possessive of her own traditions. More often than not, those invaders who landed on Chinese shores were surprised to encounter a society more developed than their own, and instead of wishing to subjugate it, ended up appropriating the country's values and practices. China, for her part, took what she considered worthwhile from foreign cultures and modified and assimilated it into her own. In this way, a mutually beneficial exchange was enacted.

The most significant external impact on the development of Chinese society was not made by would-be conquerors, however, but by tradesmen travelling the Rome-China Silk Road which was in commercial

Opposite:
China remains a country of rich contrasts and diverse cultural influences drawn from many different sources over the centuries.

use by about 100 BC. At this time, India had cultivated an equally advanced society and the trade route allowed the two civilizations to meet without hostility. This encounter brought Buddhism to China, which of any other alien influence, had perhaps the most dramatic, long-term effect on her culture and literary heritage.

In common with many other nations, both Western and Eastern, the earliest mythology of the Chinese was in the oral tradition. Myths were very rare before 800 BC when fragments of tales with an astrological theme began to gain popularity. Subsequent Chinese myths and legends fall into several distinct groups. The myths presented in the first two chapters of this book are all based on ancient tales arising from a highly fertile mythical period, up to and including the overthrow of the Yin dynasty and the establishment of the Zhou dynasty in 1122 BC. The third chapter offers a selection of popular, miscellaneous fables, spanning a number of later eras. It should be noted, however, that the period of antiquity in which these legends and fables are set is no indication of when they were actually first transcribed. The earliest myths, as we know them today, for example, the Creation Myths, have to be recognized as the reconstructions of a later, post-Confucian culture. These early tales, collected in different ancient books, such as the great historical annals, give only the most frugal biographical account of characters and events. In time, these tales were embellished with more detail, appearing in works like the Toaist *Shanghaijing (The Classic of Mountains and Seas)*, where a deeper sense of mystery and fantasy is woven around an existing historical record.

The imaginative minds of the ancient Chinese were crowded with Gods, giants, fairies, mortal heroes and devils, all of which ultimately appeared in their literature. Before Buddhism, Chinese religious practices were similar to those of the ancient Greeks, incorporating a huge number of deities who represented every aspect of nature, and a whole system of beliefs which attempted to explain the complexities of the universe in simple, human terms. The most important school of thought dominating China for thousands of years, was Confucianism[1], which devoted itself principally to the regulation of human relationships with a view to creating a practical social structure which would enable people to live in greater harmony together. Confucius favoured a more rational approach to life than that which he saw around him and discouraged the belief in the supernatural.

Co-existing with this methodical outlook, however, was the school of thought known as Taoism, seeking out the essential laws of nature which govern our lives, and in the age of Lao Tzu, the reputed founder of the Taoist religion, fresh myths began to appear. The period of the Warring States, 500 to 100 BC, again brought new impetus and greater emotional depth to mythological creation.

This era was followed by the advent of Buddhism which

Opposite: Buddhism, of any other alien influence, had perhaps the most dramatic, long-term effect on China's culture and literary heritage.

1 Please refer to the Glossary for more detail on Confucianism, Buddhism and Taoism.

introduced to China many tales adapted from Indian mythology. To combat this foreign influence, Taoists invented newer characters and legends, mixing fact and fiction to a degree where the worlds of myth and reality become indistinguishable.

Broadly speaking, the diverse influences of Confucianism, Taoism and Buddhism resulted in a literature which was firmly rooted in the concept that everything on earth was in some way subject to divine authority. Order and peace exist on earth when Heaven's authority is acknowledged, but when it is ignored, natural calamities, such as floods and drought, are set to occur. According to the Taoist view, the supreme power of Heaven is administered by celestial government officials. Compared to the other splendours of creation, the mountains and streams, the forests and flowers, man's importance is diminished. Never before, in any other culture or early literature, was the emphasis on nature and humanity's communion with it, so crucial. Man's good fortune depended on his ability to behave in accordance with the dictates of Heaven. From ancient times onwards, the highest ambition he could aspire to was to determine the natural law of things and to behave in sympathy with it.

✳   ✳   ✳

AUTHORS' NOTE

The Chinese mythological tradition has furnished us with an extensive catalogue of ancient tales, several thousand in number. This volume is intended to provide an enjoyable and entertaining introduction to the most popular of those myths and fables and is in no way a comprehensive study of its subject. Nonetheless, it is hoped that the stories included will inspire and encourage the reader to explore further the fascinating world of Chinese mythology.

CHINESE DYNASTIES

Early Mythical Rulers

Fu Xi
Shen Nung

The Five Emperors

Huang Ti (Yellow Emperor)
Shao Hao (White Emperor)
Zhuan Xu (Black Emperor)
Tai Hou (Green Emperor)
Chih Ti (Red Emperor)

Patriarchs of the Yin Nation

King Yao
Shun
The Xia Dynasty 2205 -1766 BC
Yü
The Shang (Yin) Dynasty 1766-1121 BC
Tang
The Zhou Dynasty 1121-255 BC
Wu
The Chin Dynasty 255-206 BC
Chin Shih Huang Ti
The Western Han Dynasty 206 BC-AD 25
Wang Mang the Usurper
The Eastern Han Dynasty AD 25-221
The Three Kingdoms AD 221-265
The Chin Dynasty AD 265-420
The Sung Dynasty AD 420-479
The Six Dynasties AD 470-581
The Sui Dynasty AD 581-618
The Tang Dynasty AD 618-906
The Five Dynasties AD 907-960
The Northern Sung Dynasty AD 960-1126
The Southern Sung Dynasty AD 1127-1279
The Yüan (Mongol) Dynasty AD 1260-1368
The Ming Dynasty AD 1368-1644
The Ching Dynasty AD 1644-1911

THE CREATION MYTHS

he earliest Chinese myths, believed to have evolved in the primitive society of what is now northern China, are very old indeed, some of them dating back to the eighth century BC. They were passed on by word of mouth, by a simple people attempting to explain the origins of the cosmos and other astronomical phenomena beyond their comprehension.

The story of Pan Gu, although generally considered one of China's earliest legends, is actually from a much later period. Some scholars of Chinese mythology suggest that this myth was imported from Indo-China shortly before the advent of Buddhism in the first century BC. Other scholars attribute the tale specifically to the fourth century Taoist philosopher Ko Hung, author of the *Shen Hsien Chuan (Biographies of the Gods)*.

But whatever his precise origins, the tale of how Pan Gu fashioned the universe is now very firmly established in Chinese folklore and a great number of Chinese people still trace their ancestry back to this particular god and his successor, the goddess Nü Wa. Ancient Chinese tales which centre on these two characters are commonly known as 'Creation Myths'.

Nü Wa and her consort, Fu Xi, were created to embellish the mythological notion of the origin of things. Again, the concept of Nü Wa is a very ancient one, first mentioned by Lieh Tzu in the fifth century BC. Nü Wa and Fu Xi are the great gentle protectors of humanity, while the God of Water, Gong Gong, is depicted as the destroyer of the earth. In these stories an interesting tension is introduced between the opposing forces of creativity and destruction.

Pan Gu and the Creation of the Universe

AT THE VERY BEGINNING OF TIME, when only darkness and chaos existed and the heavens and the earth had not yet been properly divided up, the universe resembled the shape of a large egg. And at the centre of this egg, the first living creature one day came into being. After many thousands of years, when he had gathered sufficient strength and energy and had grown to the size of a giant, the creature, who gave himself the name of Pan Gu, awoke fully refreshed from his long rest and stood upright within his shell. He began to yawn very loudly and to stretch his enormous limbs, and as he did so, the walls of the egg were cracked open and separated into two even portions. The lighter, more fragile, part of the egg floated delicately upwards to form the white silken sheet of the sky, while the heavier, more substantial part, dropped downwards to form the earth's crusty surface.

Now when Pan Gu observed this, he was happy and proud to have created some light in place of the darkness and chaos out of which he had emerged. But at the same time, he began to fear that the skies and the earth might fuse once more, and he stood and scratched his huge head, pondering a solution to the problem. And after he had thought things through for quite a while, he decided that the only way to keep the two elements at a safe distance from each other was to place his own great bulk between them. So he took up his position, heaving and pushing upwards against the sky with his hands and pressing downwards into the earth with all the weight of his massive feet until a reasonable gap had been formed.

For the next eighteen thousand years, Pan Gu continued to push the earth and the sky apart, growing taller and taller every day until the gap measured some thirty thousand miles. And when this distance between them had been established, the sky grew firm and solid and the earth became securely fixed far beneath it. Pan Gu then looked around him and seeing that there was no longer any danger of darkness returning to the universe, he felt at last that he could lay down and rest, for his bones ached and he had grown old and frail over the years. Breathing a heavy sigh, he fell into an exhausted sleep from which he never awoke. But as he lay dying, the various parts of his vast body were miraculously transformed to create the world as we mortals know it today.

Opposite: And when people later came to inhabit the earth, they worshipped Pan Gu as a great creator and displayed the utmost respect for all the natural elements.

Pan Gu's head became the mountain ranges; his blood became the rivers and streams; the hairs on his head were changed into colourful and fragrant blossoms and his flesh was restored to

become the trees and soil. His left eye was transformed into the sun and his right eye became the moon; his breath was revived in the winds and the clouds and his voice resounded anew as thunder and lightning. Even his sweat and tears were put to good use and were transformed into delicate droplets of rain and sweet-smelling morning dew.

And when people later came to inhabit the earth, they worshipped Pan Gu as a great creator and displayed the utmost respect for all the natural elements, believing them to be his sacred body spread out like a carpet before them beneath the blue arch of the heavens.

Nü Wa Peoples the Earth

WHEN THE UNIVERSE FIRST EMERGED from chaos, mankind had not yet been created and the firmament and all the territories beneath it were inhabited by Gods or giants who had sprung forth from the body of Pan Gu. At that time, one particularly powerful Goddess appeared on earth in the company of her chosen heavenly companion. The Goddess's name was Nü Wa and her companion's name was Fu Xi. Together these deities set out to bring an even greater sense of order and regulation to the world.

And of all the other Gods residing in the heavens, Nü Wa was the strangest and most unusual in appearance, for the upper half of her body was shaped like a human being, while the lower part took the form of a snake. Nü Wa also possessed the unique ability to change her shape up to seventy times a day and she frequently appeared on earth in several different guises.

Although Nü Wa took great pleasure in the wondrous beauty of the new-born world she occupied, deep within she felt it to be a little too silent and she yearned to create something that would fill the empty stillness. One day shortly afterwards, as she walked along the banks of the great Yellow River, she began to imagine spending time in the company of

Opposite:
Nü Wa, the successor of Pan Gu, is traditionally depicted in Chinese mythology as a half-human, half-serpent, female goddess.

other beings not unlike herself, animated creatures who might talk and laugh with her and with whom she could share her thoughts and feelings. Sitting herself down on the earth, she allowed her fingers to explore its sandy texture and without quite realizing it, began to mould the surrounding clay into tiny figures. But instead of giving

them the lower bodies of reptiles, the Goddess furnished her creatures with little legs so they would stand upright. Pleased with the result, she placed the first of them beside her on the earth and was most surprised and overjoyed to see it suddenly come to life, dancing around her and laughing excitedly. She placed another beside it and again the same thing happened. Nü Wa was delighted with herself and with her own bare hands she continued to make more and more of her little people as she rested by the river bank.

But as the day wore on, the Goddess grew tired and it was then that she decided to make use of her supernatural powers to complete the task she had begun. So breaking off a length of wood from a nearby mulberry tree, she dredged it through the water until it was coated in mud. Then she shook the branch furiously until several hundred drops of mud landed on the ground and as each drop landed it was instantly transformed into a human being. Then Nü Wa pronounced that the beings she had shaped with her own hands should live to become the rich and fortunate people of the world, while those created out of the drops of mud should lead ordinary and humble lives. And realizing that her little creatures should themselves be masters of their own survival, Nü Wa separated them into sons and daughters and declared that they should marry and multiply until the whole wide world had become their home and they were free once and for all from the threat of extinction.

The War Between the Gods of Fire and Water

FOR A GREAT MANY YEARS after Nü Wa had created human beings, the earth remained a peaceful and joyous place and it was not until the final years of the Goddess's reign that mankind first encountered pain and suffering. For Nü Wa was extremely protective of the race she had created and considered it her supreme duty to shelter it from all harm and evil. People depended on Nü Wa for her guardianship and she, in turn, enabled them to live in comfort and security.

One day, however, two of the Gods who dwelt in the heavens, known as Gong Gong and Zhurong, became entangled in a fierce and bitter dispute. No one knew precisely why the two Gods began to shout and threaten one another, but before long they were resolved to do battle against each other and to remain fighting to the bitter end.

Opposite: Nü Wa's companion on earth was called Fu Xi. Together these deities brought a greater sense of order and harmony to the world.

Gong Gong, who was the God of Water, was well known as a violent and ambitious character and his bright red wavy hair perfectly mirrored his fiery and riotous spirit. Zhurong, the God of Fire, was equally belligerent when provoked and his great height and bulk rendered him no less terrifying in appearance.

Several days of fierce fighting ensued between the two of them during which the skies buckled and shifted under the strain of the combat. An end to this savage battle seemed to be nowhere in sight, as each God thrust and lunged with increasing fury and rage, determined to prove himself more powerful than the other. But on the fourth day, Gong Gong began to weary and Zhurong gained the upper hand, felling his opponent to the ground and causing him to tumble right out of the heavens.

Crashing to the earth with a loud bang, Gong Gong soon became acutely aware of the shame and disgrace of his defeat and decided that he would never again have the courage to face any of his fellow Gods. He was now resolved to end his own life and looked around him for some means by which he might perform this task honourably and successfully. And seeing a large mountain range in the distance rising in the shape of a giant pillar to the skies, Gong Gong ran towards it with all the speed he could muster and rammed his head violently against its base.

As soon as he had done this, a terrifying noise erupted from within the mountain, and gazing upwards, Gong Gong saw that a great wedge of rock had broken away from the peak, leaving behind a large gaping hole in the sky. Without the support of the mountain, the sky began to collapse and plummet towards the earth's surface, causing great crevasses to appear on impact. Many of these crevasses released intensely hot flames which instantly engulfed the earth's vegetation, while others spouted streams of filthy water which merged to form a great ocean. And as the flood and destruction spread throughout the entire world, Nü Wa's people no longer knew where to turn to for help. Thousands of them drowned, while others wandered the earth in terror and fear, their homes consumed by the raging flames and their crops destroyed by the swift-flowing water.

Opposite: When people came to inhabit the earth they respected all the natural elements believing them to be Pan Gu's body spread out like a carpet.

Nü Wa witnessed all of this in great distress and could not bear to see the race she had created suffer such appalling misery and deprivation. Though she was now old and looking forward to her time of rest, she decided that she must quickly take action to save her people, and it seemed that the only way for her to do this was to repair the heavens as soon as she possibly could with her very own hands.

Nü Wa Repairs the Sky

NÜ WA RAPIDLY set about gathering the materials she needed to mend the great hole in the sky. One of the first places she visited in her search was the river Yangtze where she stooped down and gathered up as many pebbles as she could hold in both arms. These were carefully chosen in a variety of colours and carried to a forge in the heavens where they were melted down into a thick, gravel-like paste. Once she had returned to earth, Nü Wa began to repair the damage, anxiously filling the gaping hole with the paste and smoothing whatever remained of it into the surrounding cracks in the firmament. Then she hurried once more to the river bank and, collecting together the tallest reeds, she built a large, smouldering fire and burnt the reeds until they formed a huge mound of ashes. With these ashes Nü Wa sealed the crevasses of the earth, so that water no longer gushed out from beneath its surface and the swollen rivers gradually began to subside.

After she had done this, Nü Wa surveyed her work, yet she was still not convinced that she had done enough to prevent the heavens collapsing again in the future. So she went out and captured one of the giant immortal tortoises which were known to swim among the jagged rocks at the deepest point of the ocean and brought it ashore to slaughter it. And when she had killed the creature, she chopped off its four sturdy legs and stood them upright at the four points of the compass as extra support for the heavens. Only now was the Goddess satisfied and she began to gather round her some of her frightened people in an attempt to reassure them that order had finally been restored.

To help them forget the terrible experiences they had been put through, Nü Wa made a flute for them out of thirteen sticks of bamboo and with it she began to play the sweetest, most soothing music. All who heard it grew calmer almost at once and the earth slowly began to emerge from the chaos and destruction to which it had been subjected. From that day forth, Nü Wa's people honoured her by calling her 'Goddess of music' and many among them took great pride in learning the instrument she had introduced them to.

But even though the heavens had been repaired, the earth was never quite the same again. Gong Gong's damage to the mountain had caused the skies to tilt permanently towards the north-west so that the Pole Star, around which the heavens revolved, was dislodged from its position directly overhead. The sun and the moon were also tilted, this time in the direction of the west, leaving a great depression in the south-east. And not only that, but the peak of the mountain which had crashed to the earth had left a huge hollow where it landed in the east into which the rivers and streams of the world flowed incessantly.

Nü Wa had done all she could to salvage the earth and shortly afterwards, she died. Her body was transformed into a thousand fairies who watched over the human race on her behalf. Her people believe that the reason China's rivers flow eastwards was because of Gong Gong's foolish collision with the mountain, a belief that is still shared by their ancestors today.

❋   ❋   ❋

TALES OF THE FIVE EMPERORS

fter Nü Wa had peopled the earth, several of the heavenly gods began to take a greater interest in the world below them. The five most powerful of these gods descended to earth in due course and each was assigned various territories of the new world.

The Yellow Emperor (Huang Ti), the most important of the five sovereigns, is a part-mythical, part-historical figure who is reputed to have founded the Chinese nation around 4000 BC. During his 'historical' reign he is said to have developed a number of important astronomical instruments and mathematical theories, as well as introducing the first calendar to his people and a system for telling the time. He is always depicted as a figure who takes particular pride in humanity and one who consistently reveals a great love of nature and of peaceful existence.

Yet in order to achieve peace, the Yellow Emperor is forced, at one time or another, to battle against the other four gods. These include the Fiery or Red Emperor (Chih Ti), who is the Yellow Emperor's half-brother by the same mother, the White Emperor (Shao Hao), the Black Emperor (Zhuan Xu), and the Green Emperor (Tai Hou). The Yellow Emperor is victorious over all of these gods and he divides up the earth into four equal regions. The Red Emperor is placed in charge of the south, the White Emperor is in charge of the west, the Black Emperor rules the north, while the Green Emperor rules the east.

The Yellow Emperor's Earthly Kingdom

AFTER HE HAD GROWN for twenty-five months in his mother's womb, the infant God Huang Ti was safely delivered at last, bringing great joy to his celestial father, the God of Thunder. As soon as he appeared, Huang Ti had the gift of speech, and in each of his four faces the determination and energy of a born leader shone brightly for all to see. By the time the young God had grown to manhood, he alone among other deities had befriended every known spirit-bird, and a great many phoenixes travelled from afar simply to nest in his garden, or to perch themselves on the palace roof and terraces to serenade him with the sweetest of melodies.

When the five most powerful Gods decided to explore the earth, it was already in the minds of each that one among them should be assigned absolute and supreme control over the others. But the God of Fire, who was later known as the Red Emperor, was reluctant to share power with anyone, especially with his half-brother Huang Ti who seemed to be everyone else's natural choice. So when the time of the election came, the Red Emperor launched a vicious attack on the Yellow Emperor, instigating one of the fiercest battles the earth had ever witnessed. It was fought on the field of Banquan where the allies of Huang Ti, including wolves, leopards, bears and huge birds of prey, gathered together and rushed at the Red Emperor's troops until every last one of them lay slain.

Once this great battle was over and the Yellow Emperor had been acknowledged by all as supreme ruler, he set about building for himself a divine palace at the top of Mount Kunlun, which reached almost to the clouds. The magnificent royal residence, consisting of no less than five cities and twelve towers surrounded by solid walls of priceless jade, was flanked by nine fire-mountains which burnt day and night casting their warm red glow on the palace walls.

The front entrance faced eastwards and was guarded by the Kaiming, the loyal protector of the Gods, who had nine heads with human faces and the body of a giant panther. The exquisite gardens of the royal palace, where the Emperor's precious pearl trees and jade trees blossomed

Opposite:
Huang-Ti chose yellow as his imperial colour and built for himself a great palace on top of Mount Kunlun at the centre of the world.

all year round, were protected by the three-headed God Li Zhu who sat underneath the branches never once allowing his three heads to sleep at the same time. This God was also guardian of the dan trees which bore five different exotic fruits once every five years, to be eaten exclusively by the Emperor himself.

From the largest garden, which was known as the Hanging Garden, a smooth path wound its way upwards to the heavens so that many of the most prestigious Gods and the rarest divine beasts chose to make the Emperor's wondrous kingdom their home, content that they had discovered earthly pleasures equal to their heavenly experience. And it was here, in this garden, that the supreme ruler particularly loved to sit each evening, taking time to admire his newly discovered world just as the setting sun bathed it in a gentle golden light. As he looked below him, he saw the reviving spring of Yaoshui flowing jubilantly into the crystal-clear waters of the Yaochi Lake. To the west he saw the great Emerald trees swaying delicately in the breeze, shedding a carpet of jewels on the earth beneath them. When he looked northwards his eyes were fixed upon the towering outline of Mount Zhupi where eagles and hawks soared merrily before their rest. The Yellow Emperor saw that all of this was good and knew that he would spend many happy years taking care of the earth.

The Fiery Emperor and the First Grain

THE FIERY EMPEROR, who ruled as God of the south, had the head of an ox and the body of a human being. He was also known as the God of the Sun and although in the past he had led his people in a disastrous rebellion against the Yellow Emperor, he was still much loved by his subjects and they held him in the highest esteem. The Fiery Emperor taught mankind how to control and make constructive use of fire through the art of forging, purifying and welding metals so that eventually his subjects were able to use it for cooking, lighting and for making domestic tools and hunting weapons. In those early times, the forests were filled with venomous reptiles and savage wild animals and the Fiery Emperor ordered his people to set fire to the undergrowth to drive away these dangerous and harmful creatures. He was also the first to teach them how to plant grain, together with a whole variety of medicinal herbs that could cure any ailment which might trouble them.

It was said that when the Fiery Emperor first appeared on earth he very wisely observed that there was not enough fruit on the trees, or vegetables in the ground to satisfy the appetite of his people. Knowing that mankind was forced to eat the flesh of other living creatures, the Emperor became unhappy and quickly set about instructing his subjects in the use of the plough and other tools of the land until they learned how to cultivate the soil around them. And when he saw that the soil was ready, the Emperor called for his people to pray aloud for a new and abundant food to rise up before them out of the ground.

As the people raised their faces to the heavens, a red bird carrying nine seedlings in its beak suddenly appeared through the clouds. As it swooped to the ground it began to scatter grains on to the upturned soil. After it had done this, the Fiery Emperor commanded the sun to warm the earth and from the seeds emerged five young cereal plants which began to multiply rapidly until a vast area of land was covered with luscious vegetation.

The fruits of these plants were harvested at the close of day to fill eight hundred wicker baskets. Then the Fiery Emperor showed his people how to set up market stalls and explained to them how to keep time according to the sun in order that they might barter among themselves in the future for whatever food they lacked. But even after having provided all of this, the Fiery Emperor was still not satisfied with his work. And so, taking his divine whip, he began to lash a number of the plants, which caused them to be endowed with healing properties, and he set them aside to be used by mankind whenever disease struck. The people, overjoyed that they were so well cared for, decided that the Fiery Emperor should henceforth go by the name of the Divine Peasant and they built in his honour a giant cauldron for boiling herbs and carried it to the summit of the Shenfu Mountains where it stands to this day.

The Bird and the Sea

THE FIERY EMPEROR had three daughters whom he loved and cared for very much, but it was his youngest daughter who had always occupied a special place in his heart. She was named Nü Wa, after the great Goddess who created mankind, and like her sisters she possessed a cheerful disposition and a powerful spirit of adventure.

One day Nü Wa went out in search of some amusement and seeing a little boat moored in the tiny harbour at a short distance from the palace gates, she went towards it, untied it and jumped aboard, allowing it to carry her out over the waves of the Eastern Sea. The young girl smiled happily to see the sun sparkle on the water and the graceful gulls circling overhead, but became so preoccupied in her joy that she failed to notice she had drifted out of sight, further and further towards the centre of the ocean. Suddenly, the wind picked up speed and the waves began to crash violently against the side of the boat. There was nothing Nü Wa could do to prevent herself being tossed overboard into the foaming spray and even though she struggled with every ounce of strength to save herself, she eventually lost the fight and was sadly drowned.

Just at that time, a small jingwei bird happened to approach the place where Nü Wa had fallen. And at that moment, her spirit, resentful of the fact that life had been cut short so unfairly, rose up in anger and entered the creature. Nü Wa now lived on in the form of a bird with a speckled head, white beak and red claws, and all day long she circled the skies angrily, vowing to take revenge on the sea which had deprived her of her life and left her father grieving for his beloved child.

It was not long before she conceived of a plan to fill up the sea with anything she could find, hoping that in time there would no longer be any room left for people to drown in it. So every day the little bird flew back and forth from the land out over the Eastern ocean until she grew weary with exhaustion. In her beak she carried pebbles, twigs, feathers and leaves which she dropped into the water below. But this was no easy task, and the sea laughed and jeered at the sight of the tiny bird labouring so strenuously:

'How do you imagine you will ever complete your work,' hissed the waves mockingly. 'Never in a million years will you be able to fill up the sea with twigs and stones, so why not amuse yourself somewhere else.'

But the little jingwei would not be deterred: 'If it takes me a hundred times a million years, I will not stop what I am doing. I will carry on filling you up until the end of the world, if necessary.'

And although the sea continued to laugh even more loudly over the years, the jingwei never ceased to drop into the ocean whatever she managed to collect. Later, after she had found herself a mate and they had produced children together, a flock of jingwei birds circled above the water, helping to fill up the sea. And they continue to do so to this day in China, where their persistent courage and strength have won the admiration and applause of each and every Chinese citizen.

Tai Hou, the Green Emperor

EVEN IN THE WORLD OF DEITIES, the birth of the Green Emperor, God of the East, was judged quite an extraordinary affair. The story handed down among the other Gods was that the Emperor's mother, a beautiful young mortal named Hua Xu, lived originally in the ancient kingdom of Huaxushi, a place so remote and inaccessible, that many people had begun to question its very existence. Those who believed in this land, however, knew that its inhabitants possessed unique powers and gifts and often they were referred to as partial-Gods. They could move underwater as freely as they did above the earth, for example, and it was said that they could pass through fire without suffering any injury to the flesh. They walked through the air as easily as they walked on the ground and could see through the clouds as clearly as they could through glass.

One day the young girl Hua Xu was out walking across the northern plain of Leize, a name which means 'marshes of thunder', when she happened upon a gigantic footprint in the earth. She had never before encountered an imprint of its size and stooped to the ground to inspect it more closely. Imagining that a strange and wonderful being must have passed through the marshes, she grew very excited and found that she could not suppress the urge to compare the size of the footprint with her own. Slowly and carefully, Hua Xu placed her tiny foot in the enormous hollow and as she did so a strange vibration travelled up from the ground through the entire length of her body.

Shortly afterwards, the young girl found that she was pregnant and she was more than happy to be carrying a child, for

Opposite:
The fiery Emperor quickly set about instructing his subjects in the use of the plough until they learned how to cultivate the soil.

there was no doubt in her mind that the Gods had intervened on that strange day to bring about her condition. After nine months Hua Xu gave birth to a son who bore the face of a man and the body of a snake. The elders of the people of Huanxushi advised that he should be named Tai Hou, a name fit for a supreme being they were convinced had been fathered by the God of Thunder.

Shao Hao, Son of the Morning Star

THE EMPEROR OF THE WEST, Shao Hao, was also said to have come into being as the result of a strange and wonderful union. His mother, who was considered to be one of the most beautiful females in the firmament, worked as a weaver-girl in the Palace of Heaven. And it was always the case that after she had sat weaving the whole day, she preferred nothing better than to cruise through the Milky Way in a raft of silver that had been specially built for her use. On these occasions, she would pause for rest underneath the old mulberry tree which reached more than ten thousand feet into the skies. The branches of this tree were covered in huge clusters of shining berries, hidden from the naked eye by delicately spiced, scarlet-coloured leaves. It was a well-known fact that whoever ate the fruit of this tree would immediately receive the gift of immortality and many had jour-neyed to the centre of the Milky Way with this purpose in mind.

At that time, a very handsome young star-God named Morning Star, who was also known as Prince of the White Emperor, regularly took it upon himself to watch over these berries. Often he came and sat under the Mulberry Tree where he played his stringed instrument and sang the most enchanting songs. One evening, however, Morning Star was surprised to find his usual place occupied by a strange and beautiful maiden. Timidly, he approached her, but there was hardly any need for such caution, for as the maiden raised her head, their eyes met and the two fell in love almost instantly.

The maiden invited the young God aboard her raft and together they floated off into the night sky, along the silver river of the Milky Way down towards the earth and the waves of the sea. And as Morning Star played his magical music, the maiden carved a turtledove from a precious piece of white jade and set it on the top of the mast where it stood as a joint symbol of their mutual love and their deep

Opposite:
The son of Morning Star was named Shao Hao and it was his great destiny to become White Emperor of the western realms.

desire to be guided by each other through the various storms of life. The lovers drifted together over the earth's ocean as their immortal music echoed through the air. And from this joyful union a son was born whom the happy couple named Shao Hao, and it was the child's great destiny to become White Emperor of the western realms and to rule wisely over his people.

Zhuan Xu, Emperor of the North

THE YELLOW EMPEROR and his wife once had a son called Chang Yi who turned out to be a very disappointing and disobedient child. One day, Chang Yi committed a crime so terrible, even his own father could not bring himself to discuss it, and immediately banished his son to a remote corner of the world where he hoped he would never again set eyes on him. After a time, Chang Yi had a son of his own, a very foolish-looking creature it was said, with a long, thin neck, round, beady eyes, and a pig's snout where his mouth should have been. By some form of miracle, Chang Yi's son also managed to find a mate and eventually married a strong and wholesome woman named Ah Nu. From this marriage, the Yellow Emperor's great grandson, Zhuan Xu, was produced, a God who managed to redeem the family name and who, after a careful trial period, was appointed ruler of the earth's northern territories.

Following the Yellow Emperor's great battle against Chiyou, he began to look around for a successor, for he had grown extremely weary of the rebellion and discontent he had experienced during his long reign. His great-grandson had proven himself a faithful servant and everyone now agreed that Zhuan Xu should be the next God to ascend the divine throne.

Chiyou had brought widespread destruction and suffering to the earth which led Zhuan Xu to believe that the alliance between mortals and immortals must be dissolved to prevent an even greater disaster in the future. And so he set about the task of separating the people from the Gods and turned his attention first of all to the giant ladder which ran between heaven and earth. For in those days, it was not unusual for people to ascend the ladder to consult with the Gods when they were in trouble, and the Gods, in turn, often made regular visits to the earth's surface. Chiyou had made such a visit when he secretly plotted with the Maio tribe in the south to put an end to the Yellow Emperor's sovereignty.

The bloodshed which followed would never again be tolerated by Zhaun Xu and he enlisted the aid of two Gods in his destruction of the ladder.

With their help, the world became an orderly place once more. The God Chong was assigned control of the heavens and his task was to ensure that immortals no longer descended to earth. The God Li, together with his son Yi, were put in charge of the earth. Yi had the face of a human but his feet grew out of his head to form a fan-shaped bridge to the heavens behind which the sun and the stars set each evening. Zhaun Xu supervised the work of the other Gods and took it upon himself to re-introduce discipline to a race which had become untamed. It was said that he banished all cruel instruments of war and taught mankind respect for his own kind once again. He forbade women to stand in the path of men and severely punished a sister and brother who lived together as husband and wife.

By the time Zhuan Xu died, the world was a much more peaceful place and on the day he passed away it was said that the elements rose up in a great lament. Jagged lightning lit up the skies and thunder clouds collided furiously with each other. The north wind howled fiercely and the underground streams burst to the surface in torrents of grief. Legend has it that Zhuan Xu was swept away by the water and his upper-half transformed into a fish so that he might remain on the earth in another form, ever watchful of mankind's progress.

Chiyou Challenges the Yellow Emperor

CHIYOU WAS A FEROCIOUS and ambitious God who had begun life as an aide and companion to the young deity, Huang Ti, in the days before he had risen to become Yellow Emperor on earth. During this time, the two had become firm friends and close confidants, but as soon as Huang Ti ascended the throne, this favourable relationship came to an abrupt end. For Chiyou could not bear to see his friend achieve the success he secretly longed for, and it became his obsession to find a way to reverse this situation and take the throne for himself.

Chiyou was the eldest of seventy-two brothers, all of them huge and powerful in stature. They each spoke the language of humans, but their bodies below the neckline were those of animals with cloven feet. Their heads were made of iron and their hideous copper faces contained four repulsive eyeballs protruding from mottled foreheads. These brothers ate all kinds of food, but they particularly liked to eat stones and chunks of metal, and their special skill was the manufacture of battle weapons, including sharp lances, spears, axes, shields and strong bows.

Now Chiyou had become convinced that he could easily overthrow the Yellow Emperor and so, gathering together his brothers and other minor Gods who were discontented with the Emperor's reign, he made an arrogant and boisterous descent to earth. First of all, however, he decided to establish a reputation for himself as a great warrior and immediately led a surprise attack on the ageing Fiery Emperor, knowing that he would seize power without a great deal of effort. The Fiery Emperor, who had witnessed his fair share of war, had no desire to lead his people into a climate of further suffering and torment, and soon fled from his home, leaving the way open for Chiyou to take control of the south. Shortly after this event, one of the largest barbarian tribes known as the Miao, who had been severely punished for their misdemeanours under the Fiery Emperor's authority, decided to take their revenge against the ruling monarchy and enthusiastically joined ranks of Chiyou and his brothers.

It was not long before the Yellow Emperor received word of the disturbances in the south, and hearing that it was his old friend who led the armies to rebellion, he at first tried to reason with him. But Chiyou refused to listen and insisted on war as the only path forward. The Yellow Emperor found that he had little choice but to lead his great army of Gods, ghosts, bears, leopards and tigers to the chosen battlefield of Zhuolu and here the terrible war began in earnest.

It was in Chiyou's nature to stop at nothing to secure victory against his opponent. Every subtle trick and sudden manoeuvre, no matter how underhanded, met with his approval and he had no hesitation in using his magic powers against the enemy. When he observed that his army had not made the progress he desired, he grew impatient and conjured up a thick fog which surrounded the Yellow Emperor and his men. The dense blanket of cloud swirled around them, completely obscuring their vision and they began to stab blindly with their weapons at the thin air. Then suddenly, the wild animals who made up a large part of the Emperor's forces started to panic and to flee in every direction straight into the arms of the enemy. The Yellow Emperor looked on desperately and, realizing that he was helpless to dispel the fog himself, he turned to his ministers and pleaded for help.

Fortunately, a little God named Feng Hou was among the

Emperor's men, a deity renowned for his intelligence and inventiveness. And true to his reputation, Feng Hou began to puzzle a solution to the problem and within minutes he was able to offer a suggestion.

'I cannot banish from my mind an image of the Plough which appears in our skies at night-time and always points in the same direction,' he informed the Emperor. 'Now if only I could design something similar, we would be able to pinpoint our direction no matter which way we were forced to move through the mist.'

And so Feng Hou set to work at once, using his magic powers to assist him, and within a very short time he had constructed a device, rather like a compass, which continued to point southwards, regardless of its position. And with this incredible new instrument, the Yellow Emperor finally managed to make his way out of the fog, through to the clear skies once more.

But the battle was far from over, and the Emperor began to plan his revenge for the humiliation Chiyou had brought upon his men. At once, he summoned another of his Gods before him, a dragon-shaped deity named Ying Long, who possessed the ability to make rain at will, and commanded him to produce a great flood that would overwhelm the enemy. But Chiyou had already anticipated that the Yellow Emperor would not gladly suffer his defeat, and before the dragon had even begun to prepare himself for the task ahead, Chiyou had called upon the Master of Wind and the Master of Rain who together brought heavy rains and howling winds upon the Yellow Emperor's army, leaving them close to defeat once more.

As a last desperate measure, the Emperor introduced one of his own daughters into the battlefield. Ba was not a beautiful Goddess, but she had the power to generate tremendous heat in her body, enough heat to dry up the rain which now threatened to overcome her father's legions. So Ba stood among them and before long, the rains had evaporated from the earth and the sun began to shine brilliantly through the clouds. Its bright rays dazzled Chiyou's men which enabled Ying Long to charge forward unnoticed, and as he did so, hundreds of enemy bodies were crushed beneath his giant feet, lying scattered behind him on the plains.

Opposite: A smooth path wound its way upwards to the heavens from the Yellow Emperor's palace and many of the Gods chose to make his home their own.

And seeing this result, the Yellow Emperor managed to recover some of his dignity and pride, but his army lay exhausted and the morale of his men was very low. He was worried also that they would not be able to withstand another onslaught, for although Chiyou had retreated, the Emperor was certain he would soon return

with reinforcements. He knew that he must quickly find something to lift the spirits of his men, and after much thought it suddenly came to him. What he needed most was to fill their ears with the sound of a victory drum, a drum which would resound with more power and volume than anyone had ever before imagined possible.

'With such a drum, I would bring fear to the enemy and hope to my own men,' the Emperor thought to himself. 'Two of my finest warriors must go out on my behalf and fetch a very special skin needed to produce this instrument.'

And having decided that the great beast from the Liubo Mountain possessed the only skin which would suffice, the Yellow Emperor dispatched two of his messengers to kill the strange creature. It resembled an ox without horns, he told them, and they would find it floating on the waves of the Eastern Sea. Sometimes the beast was known to open its mouth to spit out great tongues of lightning, and its roar, it was said, was worse than that of any wild cat of the forests.

But in spite of the creature's terrifying description, the Emperor's men found the courage to capture and skin it without coming to any great harm. After they had done so, they carried the hide back to the battlefield where it was stretched over an enormous bamboo frame to create an impressively large drum. At first, the Yellow Emperor was satisfied with the result, but when his men began to beat upon it with their hands, he decided that the sound was not loud enough to please him. So again, he sent two of his finest warriors on an expedition, and this time they went in search of the God of Thunder, Lei Shen. They found the God sleeping peacefully and crept up on him to remove both his thigh bones as the Emperor had commanded them to do. With these thigh bones a suitable pair of drumsticks was made and handed over to the principal drummer who stood awaiting his signal to beat on the giant instrument.

At last, the drum was struck nine times, releasing a noise louder than the fiercest thunder into the air. Chiyou's men stood paralysed with terror and fear as all around them the earth began to quake and the mountains to tremble. But this was the opportunity the Yellow Emperor's men had waited for and they rushed forward with furious energy, killing as many of Chiyou's brothers and the Miao warriors as they could lay their hands on. And when the battlefield was stained with blood and the casualties were too heavy for Chiyou to bear much longer, he called for his remaining men to withdraw from the fighting.

Opposite: Mankind wanted to believe that the Yellow Emperor would always be with them on earth, but soon he was beckoned back to the Heavens.

Refusing to surrender to the Yellow Emperor, the defeated leader fled to the north of the country to seek the help of a group of giants who took particular delight in warfare. These giants were from a tribe known as the Kua Fu and with their help Chiyou revived the strength of his army and prepared himself for the next attack.

The Yellow Emperor Returns to the Heavens

CHIYOU HAD SPENT THREE DAYS and three nights after his defeat at the battle of Zhuolu in the kingdom of the Kua Fu giants gathering rebel forces for his ongoing war against the Yellow Emperor. Both sides, it seemed, were now evenly matched once more and Chiyou relished the thought of a return to battle. But the Yellow Emperor saw that a renewal of conflict would only result in more loss of life and he was deeply disturbed and saddened by the prospect.

On the day before the second great battle was due to commence, the Emperor was sitting deep in thought in his favourite garden at the palace of Mount Kunlun when a strange Goddess suddenly appeared before him. She told him she was the Goddess of the Ninth Heaven and that she had been sent to help him in his plight.

'I fear for the lives of my men,' the Yellow Emperor told her, 'and I long for some new battle plan that will put an end to all this bloodshed.'

So the Goddess sat down on the soft grass and began to reveal to him a number of new strategies conceived by the highest, most powerful Gods of the heavens. And having reassured the Emperor that his trouble would soon be at an end, she presented him with a shining new sword furnished of red copper that had been mined in the sacred Kunwu Mountains.

'Treat this weapon with respect,' she told him as she disappeared back into the clouds, 'and its magic powers will never fail you.'

The next morning, the Emperor returned to the battlefield armed with his new strategies and the sacred weapon the Goddess had given him. And in battle after battle, he managed to overcome Chiyou's forces until at last they were all defeated and Chiyou himself was captured alive. The evil God was dragged in manacles and chains before the Yellow Emperor, but he showed no sign of remorse for the anguish he had caused and the destruction he had brought to the earth. The Yellow Emperor shook his head sadly, knowing that he now had little option but to order his prisoner's execution. The death sentence was duly announced, but Chiyou struggled so fiercely that the shackles around his ankles and wrists were stained crimson with blood.

When it was certain that he lay dead, Chiyou's manacles were cast into the wilderness where it is said they were transformed into a forest of maple trees whose leaves never failed to turn bright red each year, stained with the blood and anger of the fallen God.

And now that relative peace had been restored to the world once more, the Yellow Emperor spent his remaining time on earth re-building the environment around him. He taught the people how to construct houses for themselves where they could shelter from the rains; he brought them the gift of music and he also introduced them to the skill of writing. Mankind wanted to believe that the Yellow Emperor would always be with them on earth, but soon a divine dragon appeared in the skies, beckoning him back to the heavens. The time had arrived for the Yellow Emperor to answer this call and to acknowledge an end to the long reign of the Gods on earth. And so in the company of his fifty officials and all the other willing immortals whose stay had also run its course, he climbed on to the dragon's back and was carried up into the sky back to the heavens to take up his position again as crowned head of the celestial realms.

✳ ✳ ✳

GIANTS IN EARLY CHINESE LEGEND

n Chinese mythology, the earthly home, or 'Place of the Giant People', was said to have been in the region of the east sea, close to the Dayan Mountains. On top of Bogu Mountain lived the descendants of the dragons, giants who grew in the womb for thirty-six years before emerging fully matured and usually covered in long black hair. They could be up to fifty feet in height, with footprints six feet in length. Like their winged ancestors, they could fly before walking, and some lived as long as eighteen thousand years.

Xing Tian, the Headless Giant

ONCE THERE WAS A GIANT named Xing Tian who was full of ambition and great plans for his future. At one time, he had been an official of the Fiery Emperor, but when Chiyou had conquered the region, he had quickly switched loyalties and offered his services to the new, corrupt usurper of the south. It greatly disturbed the giant to hear reports of the bloody deaths of Chiyou's men at the hands of the Yellow Emperor and he wanted nothing less than to meet the Emperor face to face and challenge him to single combat until one of them lay dead.

So Xing Tian took up his axe and his shield and set off for the divine palace at the top of Mount Kunlun, seething with anger and rage as he thundered along. But the Yellow Emperor had received word of the giant's approach and seized his most precious sword ready to meet him head on. For days the two battled furiously, lashing out savagely with their weapons as they fought into the clouds and down the side of the mountain. They fought along all the great mountain ranges of northern China until eventually they reached the place known as the Long Sheep range in the north-east.

And it was here that the Yellow Emperor caught the giant off-guard and, raising his sword high into the air just at the level of the giant's shoulder, he slashed sideways with his blade until he had sliced off Xing Tian's head. A terrifying scream escaped the gaping, bloody mouth of the giant as his head began to topple forward, crashing with a loud thud to the ground and rolling down the hill like a massive boulder.

The giant stood frozen in absolute horror, and then he began feeling desperately with his hands around the hole above his shoulders where his head ought to have been. Soon panic had taken control of him and he thrashed about wildly with his weapon, carving up trees and tossing huge rocks into the air until the valleys began to shake and the sky began to cloud over with dust from the debris.

Seeing the giant's great fury, the Yellow Emperor grew fearful that Xing Tian might actually find his head and put it back on his shoulders again. So he swiftly drew his sword and sliced open the mountain underneath which the head had finally come to rest. Then he kicked the head into the chasm and sealed up the gap once more.

For ten thousand years afterwards the giant roamed the mountainside searching for his head. But in all that time he never

Opposite:
Even after the loss of his head, Xing Tang lived on for a great many years, determined that he would not be beaten by the Yellow Emperor.

found what he was looking for although he remained defiant that he would one day face the Yellow Emperor again. Some people say that the giant grew to be very resourceful, and to help him in his long search he used his two breasts for eyes and his navel for a mouth.

Kua Fu Chases the Sun

THE UNDERWORLD of the north where the most ferocious giants had lived since the dawn of time was centred around a wild range of black mountains. And underneath the tallest of these mountains the giant Kua Fu, gatekeeper of the dark city, had built for himself a home. Kua Fu was an enormous creature with three eyeballs and a snake hanging from each ear, yet in spite of his intimidating appearance he was said to be a fairly good-natured giant, though not the most intelligent of his race.

Kua Fu took great pleasure in everything to do with the sun. He loved to feel its warm rays on his great body, and nothing delighted him more than to watch the golden orb rise from its bed in the east each morning. He was never too keen, however, to witness it disappear below the horizon in the evenings and longed for the day when the sun would not have to sleep at night.

And as he sat watching the sun descend in the sky one particular evening, Kua Fu began thinking to himself:

'Surely I can do something to rid the world of this depressing darkness. Perhaps I could follow the sun and find out where it hides itself at night. Or better still, I could use my great height to catch it just as it begins to slide towards the west and fix it firmly in the centre of the sky so that it never disappears again.'

So the following morning, Kua Fu set off in pursuit of the sun, stepping over mountains and rivers with his very long legs, all the time reaching upwards, attempting to grab hold of the shining sphere above him. Before long, however, evening had approached, and the sun began to glow a warm red, bathing the giant in a soothing, relaxing heat. Puffing and panting with exhaustion, Kua Fu stretched his huge frame to its full length in a last great effort to seize his prize. But as he did so, he was overcome by an unbearable thirst, the like of which he had never experienced before. He raced at once to a nearby stream and drank its entire contents down in one mouthful. Still his thirst had not been quenched, so he proceeded to the

Weishui River and again gulped down the water until the river ran dry. But now he was even more thirsty and he felt as if he had only swallowed a single drop.

He began to chase all over the earth, pausing at every stream and lake, seeking to drown the fiery heat that raged within his body. Nothing seemed to have any effect on him, though he had by now covered a distance of eight thousand miles, draining the waters from every possible source he encountered. There was, however, one place that he had not yet visited where surely he would find enough water to satisfy him. That place was the great lake in the province of Henan where it was said the clearest, purest water flowed from the mountain streams into the lake's great cavern.

The giant summoned all his remaining strength and plodded along heavily in the direction of this last water hole. But he had only travelled a short distance before he collapsed to the ground, weak with thirst and exhaustion. The last golden rays of the sun curved towards his outstretched body, softening the creases on his weary forehead, and melting away his suffering. Kua Fu's eyelids began to droop freely and a smile spread its way across his face as he fell into a deep, deep, eternal sleep.

At dawn on the following morning, the sun rose as usual in the east, but the sleeping figure of the giant was no longer anywhere to be seen. In its place a great mountain had risen up towards the sky. And on the western side of the mountain a thick grove of trees had sprung up overnight. These trees were laden with the ripest, most succulent peaches whose sweet juices had the power to quench the most raging thirst of any passer-by. Many believe that the giant's body formed this beautiful site and that is why it is still named Kua Fu Mountain in his honour.

❋   ❋   ❋

MYTHS OF
OTHER GODS AND
THE YIN NATION

he stories of this chapter centre on the adventures of some of the most popular heroes of the ancient Yin nation, from Dijun and Xihe, to Yi, the indomitable archer; from Yao, the wise and benevolent Emperor, to Yü, the saviour of the human race. The welfare of the people is the dominant concern of Yao's reign, and the struggle to maintain order on earth when it is threatened by the hasty intervention of angry gods, or the foolish behaviour of lesser deities, is a recurring theme in these tales.

As with the earlier stories, many of the figures presented here are reputed to be genuinely historical. More often than not, however, characters are endowed with superhuman strength and magical skills, typical of the Chinese mythological tradition of blending fact and fiction, myth and history. Yü, for example, who succeeds Yao to the throne after the brief reign of Emperor Shun (2205-2197 BC) is an outstanding legendary hero, who first appears in the shape of a giant dragon and controls the great floodwaters on earth. He is at the same time, however, the historical founder of the Xia Dynasty, a powerful leader of the Chinese nation, ultimately responsible for the division of China into nine provinces.

Aside from these great legends, the mythological world of the Chinese is peopled by a multitude of gods and immortals, too large in number to describe here. The end of this chapter offers a brief account of the most popular of this group, among them the Eight Immortals, the Kitchen God, the Goddess of Mercy and other lesser gods of distinction.

The Ten Suns of Dijun and Xihe

THE GOD OF THE EAST, Dijun, had married the Goddess of the Sun, Xihe, and they lived together on the far eastern side of the world just at the edge of the great Eastern Ocean. Shortly after their marriage, the Goddess gave birth to ten suns, each of them a fiery, energetic, golden globe, and she placed the children lovingly in the giant Fusang tree close to the sea where they could frolic and bathe whenever they became overheated.

Each morning before breakfast, the suns took it in turns to spring from the enormous tree into the ocean below in preparation for their mother's visit when one of them would be lifted into her chariot and driven across the sky to bring light and warmth to the world. Usually the two remained together all day until they had travelled as far as the western abyss known as the Yuyuan. Then, when her sun had grown weary and the light had begun to fade from his body, Xihe returned him to the Fusang tree where he slept the night peacefully with his nine brothers. On the following morning, the Goddess would collect another of her suns, sit him beside her in her chariot, and follow exactly the same route across the sky. In this way, the earth was evenly and regularly heated, crops grew tall and healthy, and the people rarely suffered from the cold.

But one night, the ten suns began to complain among themselves that they had not yet been allowed to spend an entire day playing together without at least one of them being absent. And realizing how unhappy this situation made them feel, they decided to rebel against their mother and to break free of the tedious routine she insisted they follow. So the next morning, before the Goddess had arrived, all ten of them leapt into the skies at once, dancing joyfully above the earth, intent on making the most of their forbidden freedom. They were more than pleased to see the great dazzling light they were able to generate as they shone together, and made a solemn vow that they would never again allow themselves to become separated during the daytime.

The ten suns had not once paused to consider the disastrous consequences of their rebellion on the world below. For with ten powerful beams directed at the earth, crops began to wilt, rivers began to dry up, food became scarce and people began to suffer burns and wretched hunger pangs. They prayed for rains to drive away the suns, but none appeared. They called upon the great sorceress Nu Chou to perform her acts of magic, but her spells had no effect. They hid beneath the great trees of the forests for shade, but these were stripped of leaves and offered little or no protection. And now great hungry beasts of prey and dreaded monsters emerged from the wilderness and began to devour the human beings they encountered, unable to satisfy their huge appetites any longer. The destruction spread to every corner of the earth and the people were utterly miserable and filled with despair. They turned to their Emperor for help, knowing he was at a loss to know what to do, but he was their only hope, and they prayed that he would soon be visited by the God of Wisdom.

Yi, the Archer, is Summoned

DIJUN AND XIHE were horrified to see the effect their unruly children were having upon the earth and pleaded with them to return to their home in the Fusang tree. But in spite of their entreaties, the ten suns continued on as before, adamant that they would not return to their former lifestyle. Emperor Yao now grew very impatient, and summoning Dijun to appear before him, he demanded that the God teach his suns to behave. Dijun heard the Emperor's plea but still he could not bring himself to raise a hand against the suns he loved so dearly. It was eventually settled between them, however, that one of Yao's officials in the heavens, known as Yi, should quickly descend to earth and do whatever he must to prevent any further catastrophe.

Yi was not a God of very impressive stature, but his fame as one of the most gifted archers in the heavens was widespread, for it was well known that he could shoot a sparrow down in full flight from a distance of fifty miles. Now Dijun went to meet with Yi to explain the problem his suns had created, and he handed the archer a new red bow and a quiver of white arrows and advised him what he must do.

'Try not to hurt my suns any more than you need to,' he told Yi, 'but take this bow and ensure that you bring them under control. See to it that the wicked beasts devouring mankind are also slain and that order and calm are restored once more to the earth.'

Yi readily accepted this challenge and, taking with him his wife Chang E, he departed the Heavenly Palace and made his descent to the world below. Emperor Yao was overjoyed to see the couple approach and immediately organized a tour of the land for them, where Yi witnessed for himself the devastation brought about by Dijun's children, as he came face to face with half-burnt, starving people roaming aimlessly over the scorched, cracked earth.

And witnessing all of this terrible suffering, Yi grew more and more furious with the suns of Dijun and it slipped his mind entirely that he had promised to treat them leniently. 'The time is now past for reasoning or persuasion,' Yi thought to himself, and he strode to the highest mountain, tightened the string of his powerful bow and took aim with the first of his arrows. The weapon shot up into the sky and travelled straight through the centre of one of the suns, causing it to erupt into a thousand sparks as it split open and spun out of control to the ground, transforming itself on impact into a strange three-legged raven.

Now there were only nine suns left in the sky and Yi fitted the next arrow to his bow. One after another the arrows flew through the air, expertly hitting their targets, until the earth slowly began to cool down. But when the Emperor saw that there were only two suns left in the sky and that Yi had already taken aim, he wisely remembered that at least one sun should survive to brighten the earth and so he crept up behind the archer and stole the last of the white arrows from his quiver.

Having fulfilled his undertaking to rid Emperor Yao of the nine suns, Yi turned his attention to the task of hunting down the various hideous monsters threatening the earth. Gathering a fresh supply of arrows, he made his way southwards to fight the man-eating monster of the marsh with six feet and a human head, known as Zao Chi. And with the help of his divine bow, he quickly overcame the creature, piercing his huge heart with an arrow of steel. Travelling northwards, he tackled a great many other ferocious beasts, including the nine-headed monster, Jiu Ying, wading into a deep, black pool and throttling the fiend with his own bare hands. After that, he moved onwards to the Quingqiu marshes of the east where he came upon the terrible vulture Dafeng, a gigantic bird of unnatural strength with a wing span so enormous that whenever the bird took to the air, a great typhoon blew up around it. And on this occasion, Yi knew that his single remaining arrow would only wound the bird, so he tied a long black cord to the shaft of the arrow before taking aim. Then as the creature flew past, Yi shot him in the chest and even though the vulture pulled strongly on the cord as it attempted to make towards a place of safety, Yi dragged it to the ground, plunging his knife repeatedly into its breast until all life had gone from it.

Opposite:
Yi was not a God of impressive stature, but he could shoot a sparrow down in full flight from a distance of fifty miles.

All over the earth, people looked upon Yi as a great hero, the God who had single-handedly rescued them from destruction. Numerous banquets and ceremonial feasts were held in his honour,

all of them attended by the Emperor himself, who could not do enough to thank Yi for his assistance. Emperor Yao invited Yi to make his home on earth, promising to build him the a very fine palace overlooking Jade Mountain, but Yi was anxious to return to the heavens in triumph where he felt he rightly belonged and where, in any event, Dijun eagerly awaited an account of his exploits.

Chang E's Betrayal

AFTER YI, THE GREAT ARCHER, had returned to the heavens with his wife, he immediately went in search of the God Dijun to report on the success of his mission on earth. He had managed to save mankind from the evil destruction of the ten suns, as Dijun had requested him, and was still basking in the glory of this mammoth achievement. Yi fully expected a reception similar to the one he had been given on earth, but instead he found an angry and unforgiving God waiting to receive him. Dijun did not welcome the archer with open arms, but walked forward and spoke only a few harsh words.

'I feel no warmth or gratitude in my heart towards you,' he said to Yi in the bitterest of voices, 'you have murdered all but one of my suns, and now I cannot bear to have you in my sight. So I have decided that from this day forth, you and your wife will be banished to the earth to live among the mortals you appear to have enjoyed serving so well. Because of the foul deed you have committed, it is my judgment that you no longer merit the status of Gods and neither of you will ever be permitted to enter the Heavens again.'

And although Yi argued against his sentence, Dijun would not listen to a single word of his plea. Slowly, the archer made his way homewards, shocked and saddened by the breach of friendship and weighted down by the certain knowledge that his wife would not react well to the news.

And as expected, when Chang E had been told that she and her husband had been exiled to the earth, she was absolutely furious. Much more so than Yi, she revelled in the pleasures and privileges the Gods alone enjoyed, and throughout their married life together, she had never attempted to hide the fact that she had little or no tolerance for the inferior company of mortals. Now she began to regret ever tying herself in matrimony to the archer, for she felt strongly that she was being unduly punished for his hot-headed behaviour. Surely her banishment was totally unjust! And why was it that she was being punished for her husband's foolish actions? These thoughts circled around her head as she reluctantly gathered up her things, and she promised herself that she would never cease to reproach Yi, or allow him a day's rest, until he had made amends for what he had done to her.

The couple's earthly home was as comfortable as Yi could make it and all day long he trudged through the forests in search of the luxuries his wife demanded – the tenderest deer-flesh, or the most exotic, sun-ripened berries. But often when he would return exhausted with these items, Chang E would fling them away, declaring that she had no appetite for unsophisticated mortal food. And then she would begin to bemoan their dreadful misfortune, over and over again, while Yi sat there gloomily, his head in his hands, wishing that he had never set eyes on the suns of Dijun.

One evening, when Chang E had been thinking particularly long and hard about her miserable existence on earth, she went and stood before her husband and announced that she had made firm plans for their future.

'I have had more than enough of this wretched place,' she told Yi, 'and I have no intention of dying here like a mortal and descending to the Underworld afterwards. If you want to keep me, Yi, you must do what I ask of you and go to the west, to the Mountain of Kunlun. For I have heard that the Queen Mother of the West, who lives there, keeps a very special substance. People call it the elixir of immortality and it is said that whoever takes this potion will be granted eternal life.'

Now Yi had also heard a report of this strange queen and her magic medicine, and noticing that some of the old sparkle danced in his wife's eyes as she spoke about it, he could not find it in his heart to refuse her this request even though he knew that the journey ahead would be a treacherous one. For the Queen Mother of the West lived close to the earthly palace of the Yellow Emperor, a region encircled by fire mountains and a deep moat filled with boiling, hissing water which no mortal had ever yet penetrated. The Queen herself may have had the human face of a woman, but her teeth, it was said, were those of a tiger and her hair was long and matted, covering her ugly, scaly body which ended in a leopard's tail.

It was fortunate for Yi that he still possessed some of his God-like powers, since these enabled him to pass through the scorching flames and to swim through the intense heat of the water without coming to any harm. And having reached the opening of the cave where the queen rested, he decided that the best way to approach her was to greet her openly and

CHINESE MYTHS & LEGENDS

honestly and tell her his story from start to finish in the hope that she might help him.

To the archer's immense relief, the Queen Mother of the West listened to all he had to say with an open mind, and certainly the image he painted of his innocent wife forced to suffer equal hardship because of what he had done, invited a genuine heartfelt sympathy. The queen suddenly reached into a copper box close by and withdrew a small leather pouch which she handed to Yi.

'The magic medicine inside of this pouch is very precious indeed,' she told him. 'It has been collected from the immortal trees on Mount Kunlun which flower only every three thousand years and bear fruit only every six thousand years. If two people eat this amount, which is all I have to give you, they will both have eternal life in the world of men. But if only one person swallows it all, that person will have the complete immortality of the Gods. Now take the medicine away with you and guard it well, for its value is beyond all measure.'

And so Yi returned to his home and to his anxious wife, feeling as if a great burden had been lifted from his shoulders. For the first time in many years, his wife appeared happy to see him and she kissed his cheek as he presented her with the pouch and began to relate the entire story of his adventure, including everything the queen had told him about the magic potion. Chang E agreed with her husband that they should prepare a great feast to celebrate the end to their mortal lives and she took it upon herself to guard the medicine while her husband went in search of something very special for them to eat.

But as soon as Yi had disappeared into the trees, Chang E began to stare at the little pouch and her thoughts travelled to the days when she lived among the Gods in Heaven, breathing in the scent of beautiful flowers or reclining in the warm sunshine listening to the soothing tones of immortal music drifting gently on the breeze. A deep resentment against her husband rose up within her as she indulged this daydream of a divine kingdom she considered her rightful home and she knew that she would never be content simply with eternal life on earth. She could not let go of what Yi had

Opposite:
Dijun banished the archer and his wife to earth to live among mortals and forbade them to enter the heavens ever again.

trustingly told her, that there was only enough elixir to make one of them fully immortal again, and now she allowed her selfish desire to overcome her. Without hesitating a moment longer, Chang E quickly opened up the pouch and swallowed the entire contents all at once.

The effect of the medicine was almost immediate and Chang E felt her body become lighter and lighter until her feet began to lift themselves off the ground as they had done in the past so many times before.

'How glorious it is to be a Goddess again,' she thought to herself as she floated happily towards the flickering stars in the direction of the heavens. She rose higher and higher through the air until the earth below resembled a tiny egg and the skies around her were completely silent and still. But now a sudden fear told hold of the Goddess, for it began to dawn on her that she was entirely alone, cut off from her husband Yi and other earthly mortals, yet not safely arrived in the world of deities. And as she thought more about her return to the Heavens it occurred to her for the first time that she may not necessarily receive a warm welcome there.

'How can I confront these other Gods,' she said to herself, 'when they will certainly scorn me for taking all of the elixir myself and for abandoning my poor husband. Perhaps it is not such a good idea to return straight to Heaven.'

Chang E gazed around her and saw that she had must make an unhappy choice, either to return to the unwelcoming, grey earth, or move onwards towards the cold, silvery moon. 'It is probably quite lonely on the moon,' she thought, 'still, it seems the best place to go to for a short length of time until the Gods have forgotten my crime.' And so, she floated off towards the moon, determined that she would move on from here before too long.

But the moon was far more desolate and dispiriting than she had imagined possible, a cold, hostile place, totally uninhabited, apart from one rabbit who sat forlornly under a cassia tree. Chang E could not bear it a moment longer, and having decided that even a host of angry Gods presented a more desirable alternative, she attempted to rise again into the air. But she soon discovered that her powers had deserted her and that a strange metamorphosis was taking place in her body. Her back stiffened suddenly and then curved forwards. Her breasts separated and flattened, causing her stomach to bulge outwards. Small swellings began to appear all over her skin which lost its translucence and changed to a dull, murky green.

Her mouth stretched wider and wider to the edge of her face where her ears once rested and her eyes grew larger and larger until they formed two ugly black rounds.

Once a beautiful and faithful wife, the greedy and disloyal Chang E had finally met with her punishment and was transformed

into a giant toad. And in this form she remained until the end of time, doomed to keep a lonely watch over the earth below while yearning, every passing moment, to be with the husband she had so falsely deceived.

Hou-Ji, the Ice-Child

JIANG YUAN was one of four wives of Di Ku, God of the East. For many years the couple had tried to have a child together but they had not been successful and their marriage was not a very happy one as a result. One day, however, Jiang Yaun was walking along by the riverbank when she spotted a trail of large footprints in the earth. She was intrigued by them and began to follow where they led, placing her own tiny feet in the hollows of the ground. She was unaware that by doing this, she would conceive a child, and not long afterwards she gave birth to a son, an event which under normal circumstances would have brought her great joy.

But Jiang Yuan was filled with shame to see the tiny bundle wriggling in her arms, knowing that she had absolutely no knowledge of its father. And realizing that she would have great difficulty explaining the infant's birth to her husband, Jiang Yaun made up her mind to dispose of the child before she became a victim of scandalous gossip and derision. So she took the baby to a deserted country lane and left him to perish in the cold among the sheep and cattle. But then a strange thing happened. For instead of rejecting the baby and trampling him to death, the sheep and cattle treated him as one of their own, carrying him to a nearby barn where they nestled up close to him to keep him warm and suckled him with their own milk until he grew fit and strong.

Now Jiang Yuan had sent her scouts into the countryside to make sure that her unwanted child no longer lived. The news that he had survived and that he was being cared for by the animals of the pastures threw her into a fit of rage and she ordered her men to take the infant deep into the forests, to the most deserted spot they could find, where he was to be abandoned without any food or water. Jiang Yuan's messengers performed their duty exactly as they had been commanded, but again, fate intervened to save the child.

For one morning, a group of woodcutters who had travelled into the heart of the forest to find sturdier trees, spotted the child crawling through the undergrowth. Alarmed by his nakedness and grimy appearance, they immediately swept him up off the ground and carried him back to their village. Here, the woman Chingti, who was herself without child, took charge of the infant. She wrapped him in warm clothing and filled him with nourishing food until gradually he grew plump and healthy. His foster-mother doted on her son and it brought her great pleasure to see him thrive in her care.

But again, Jiang Yuan managed to track down the child and this time she was resolved to stop at nothing until she was certain of his destruction. And so, as a last resort, she carried him herself to a vast frozen river in the north where she stripped him naked and threw him on to the ice. For two years, the infant remained on the frozen waters, but from the very first day, he was protected from the piercing cold by a flock of birds who took it in turn to fly down with morsels of food and to shelter him under their feathered wings.

The people grew curious to know why the birds swooped on to the icy surface of the river every day when clearly there were no fish to be had. Eventually a group of them set off across the ice to investigate further and soon they came upon the young child, curled up against the warm breast of a motherly seagull. They were amazed at the sight and took it as a sign that the child they had discovered was no ordinary mortal, but a very precious gift from the Gods. They rescued the young boy and named him Hou-Ji and as they watched him grow among them, his outstanding talents began to manifest themselves one by one.

Hou-Ji became an excellent farmer in time, but he did not follow any conventional model. He was a born leader and from a very early age he had learned to distinguish between every type of cereal and edible grain. He made agricultural tools for the people, such as hoes and spades, and soon the land delivered up every variety of crop, including wheat, beans, rice and large, succulent wild melons. The people had a bountiful supply of food and when the Emperor himself heard of Hou-Ji's great work he appointed him a minister of the state so that his knowledge of agriculture would spread throughout the nation.

When Hou-Ji died he left behind a 'Five-Crop-Stone' which guaranteed the Chinese people a constant supply of food even in times of famine. He was buried on the Duguang Plain, a magnificent region of rolling hills and clear-flowing rivers where the land has always remained exceptionally fertile.

Gun Battles the Great Flood

KING YAO, the first mortal emperor of China, was judged an outstanding monarch by his subjects, one of the wisest, most devoted rulers that had ever risen to power. Humble and charitable almost to a fault, Yao never allowed himself luxuries of any kind. He wore sackcloth in summer and only a deerskin during the winter months and spent his entire life making sure that his people had everything they could possibly need to keep them satisfied. If the Emperor spotted a man without clothes, he would remove the shirt from his own back and hand it over to the unfortunate person. If his people were short of food, he blamed himself for their suffering. If they committed a crime, he was immediately understanding and took personal responsibility for the breach of law and order.

Yet in spite of Yao's remarkably warm and tolerant nature, he was destined to suffer repeated misfortunes during his lifetime and his reign was plagued by disasters of every kind, including drought, starvation, disease and floods. But perhaps the worst period of the Emperor's rule came immediately after he had rid the earth of the suns of Dijun, when he had just breathed a sigh of relief and had set to work restoring the shattered morale of his nation.

During these days immediately following the destruction of the suns, when chaos still ruled the earth and the world of mortals failed to communicate a peaceful and harmonious atmosphere, the High God, Tiandi, happened to peer down from the Heavens and began to shake his head disappointedly. Everywhere the God looked, he saw people living miserable and wretched lives. Flames had devoured the homes of many and now they squabbled bitterly among themselves, desperate to secure basic food and provisions even by the most dishonest means.

Now Tiandi was not a God renowned for his patience and he saw only that mankind had begun to tread a path of wickedness and corruption. And taking swift action, he sent the God of Water to the earth's surface, commanding him to create a flood that would punish mankind for its debauched behaviour. This flood, he announced, would last for a period of no less than twenty-two years, after which time, it was hoped that the world would be properly cleansed of all evil.

So day after day the rains beat down upon the soil, pulverizing the crops which remained, flooding the houses, swelling the rivers to bursting point, until eventually the whole of the earth resembled one

Opposite:
A large and mighty dragon sprung forth from the body of Gun. It was his son Yü, destined to complete his father's unfinished work.

vast ocean. Those who were fortunate enough to avoid drowning, floated on the treacherous waters in search of tall trees or high mountains where they might come to rest. But even if they managed to reach dry land, they were then forced to compete with the fiercest beasts of the earth for food, so that many were mercilessly devoured even as they celebrated the fact that they had been saved.

Only one God among the deities of the heavens appeared to feel any sympathy for the innocent people suffering such appalling misery on earth. The God's name was Gun and he was the grandson of the Yellow Emperor. Now Gun took it upon himself to plead with Tiandi to put an end to the heavy rains, but the High God would not listen to a word of what he had to say and so Gun was forced to continue roaming the heavens, powerless to help the drowning people.

One day, however, as the young God sat alone dejectedly, pondering the destruction caused by the ongoing flood, he was approached by two of his friends, an eagle and a tortoise. And seeing their companion so downcast, the two enquired what they might do to lift his spirits.

'The only thing that would make me happy right now,' Gun answered them, 'would be to stop this water pouring out of the skies. But I have no idea how I can bring this about.'

'It is not such a difficult task,' replied the eagle, 'if you feel you have courage enough to pay a visit to Tiandi's palace. For he is the keeper of the Shirang, a very precious substance which has exactly the same appearance of soil or clay. But if you can manage to drop some of this magical clay into the ocean, it will swell up to form a great dam that will hold back the flood waters.'

It remains a great mystery to this day precisely how Gun overcame every obstacle to retrieve a handful of the magic soil, but he managed this task successfully and immediately departed for the earth where he flung the clay into the ocean. Almost at once, mountains began to spring up from the water and soon great stretches of land appeared everywhere as the huge waves began to subside. Filled with gratitude, the gaunt-faced people crawled down from the trees and out of their remote hiding places and began to hail Gun as the saviour of mankind.

But the High God, Tiandi, was not at all pleased with Gun's theft of the Shirang and its subsequent healing effect on the world below. Enraged by this challenge to his authority, he ordered the God of Fire, Zhurong, to go down to earth to murder the God who had betrayed him. The two met in combat on Mount Yushan, but Gun was no match for Zhurong and the God of Fire quickly overcame his opponent, striking him down without difficulty after they had exchanged only a few blows. And now the flood waters burst through the dam Gun had created, crashing on to the dried-out earth which became completely submerged once again.

Gun had sacrificed his life on Mount Yushan for the good of mankind, but he had died without completing his work and so his spirit refused to rest within the shell of his dead body. For three years, his remains lay in a special vault in the mountains, watched over by the people who greatly mourned his loss. But in all this time, Gun's body showed no sign of decomposing, for a new life had begun to grow inside of him, waiting for the day when it would be mature enough to emerge.

After these three years had passed and Gun's body had still not wasted away, Tiandi grew very concerned, fearing that the dead God was being transformed into an evil spirit destined to plague him for the rest of his days. So Tiandi sent one of his most trusted officials down to earth to carve up Gun's remains, presenting him with a divine sword called the Wudao. But a fantastic thing occurred as soon as the official's blade had slashed open Gun's belly. For instead of the blood he had anticipated would emerge from the opening, a large and mighty golden dragon sprung forth in its place. This dragon was Yü, the son of Gun, who had inherited all the strength and courage of his father and who had entered the world in all his magnificent glory to complete Gun's unfinished work.

Yü Controls the Flood

THE APPEARANCE OF a great golden dragon in the skies, whose sole purpose it was to save mankind from destruction, encouraged the High God, Tiandi, to question whether or not the punishment he had meted out to the people below had been a little too severe. The mysterious creature was fiercely determined and persistent, he noticed, and to allow any further grievances between them was not the most prudent way forward. So Tiandi decided to yield to the dragon's wishes and put an end to the suffering on earth at long last.

Yü's mission so far had been an easy one. Tiandi not only ordered the God of Water to call a halt to the downpour, he also gave Yü enough Shirang to construct another great dam to hold back the flood waters. He sent the dragon Ying Long down to earth to assist him in repairing the widespread damage. Yü received this help gratefully and day and night channelled all his available energy into the task at hand.

Now all would have gone on smoothly, and the earth been restored to its original condition in little or no time, but for the God of Water, Gong Gong, who decided to cause as much trouble as possible for Yü. For it was Gong Gong who had originally created the flood and to see his great work undone by a mere boy-dragon was more than he could tolerate. No one had yet dared to disobey Yü's commands, but Gong Gong ignored every last one of them, entirely underestimating the dragon's strength and the powerful influence he exerted over his followers. And seeing that Gong Gong would not be reasoned with, Yü called together all the fairies, spirits and giants of the earth, so that not one remained to fight alongside Gong Gong. Then Yü challenged the God of Water to single combat, an encounter Gong Gong now wished he could avoid, for in no time, Yü had defeated him and skewered his ugly head upon his sword.

And after he had vanquished the God of Water, Yü went among the people handing them pieces of the magic clay so that they could decide for themselves where mountain ranges should appear and where stretches of land would flourish most. But it was not enough simply to rebuild the earth again, nor was the giant dam a permanent safeguard against flooding in the future. Yü realized that something more had to be done and so, dragging his great tail in the earth, he began to hollow out the soil, digging a long, tunnel-like structure through which the water could easily and swiftly flow, away from the land in the direction of the sea. Throughout the country, people followed his example and soon an entire network of shallow gullies began to appear, draining the surplus water from the plains. In this way, Yü brought the flood under control and created the great rivers of China that still flow eastwards towards the ocean to this very day.

The Marriage of Yü

Opposite:
According to the song of the strange white fox, Nu Jiao, who dwelt in the distant valley of Tu, was destined to become Yü's wife.

YÜ HAD SPENT THIRTY YEARS on earth regulating the waters before it even occurred to him that he had earned a well-deserved rest and that perhaps the time had now arrived to make plans for his own future. Never in the past had he paused to consider the possibility that he might one day marry, but suddenly he felt lonely and in need of a wife

who could love him and attend to him in old age. He had no idea how he might go about choosing a wife, however, and decided to put his trust in the Gods, waiting patiently for a sign from the divine powers above.

One morning, he observed a strange white fox with nine tails making its way towards him and he felt at once that the animal must be a heavenly messenger sent to help him in his quest. The fox approached and began to sing a strange little song which Yü listened to attentively, confident that its words would somehow enlighten him. The fox's song cheered him immensely and left him in little doubt that his search for a suitable wife was drawing to a close:

> *He who meets with the fox of nine tails*
> *Will soon become king of the land.*
> *He who weds the chief's daughter on Mount Tu*
> *Will become a prosperous man.*

Nu Jiao was reputed to be one of the most beautiful maidens in China and she dwelt in the distant valley of Tu on the summit of the great mountain. Ever since childhood, she had heard nothing but favourable reports of Yü and by now she was familiar with everything he had accomplished on earth. She had come to admire him from a distance as a God of legendary stature, and in her heart she had always entertained the hope that one day they would meet. And so when Yü appeared unexpectedly and asked for her hand in marriage, Nu Jiao could scarcely believe her good fortune and agreed at once to become his bride.

The two departed her father's kingdom and travelled southwards where they set up home and began a very happy married life together. It was not long before Nu Jiao became pregnant and the couple were overjoyed at the prospect of a son who would carry on his father's good work. For although the majority of the floods had been checked, the task of clearing the debris and ensuring that no similar disasters occurred in the future was still very much incomplete. And as the days passed by, the responsibility of overseeing more and more of this kind of work fell on Yü's experienced shoulders. Often he was forced to spend days away from home and occasionally he was away for several weeks at a time.

Now when the time was close at hand for Nu Jiao to deliver her child, Yü was unfortunately summoned to help restore the Huanyan Mountain which had begun to collapse and slide treacherously into the sea.

And knowing that his wife would be anxious during his absence, Yü offered her the following words of comfort:

'If the task ahead were not so dangerous I would allow you to accompany me,' he told her. 'But I won't be very far away and I will take this drum with me and beat on it loudly when it is safe for you to join me.'

Nu Jiao was relieved to hear this and she bade her husband farewell and watched him disappear into the forest.

As soon as he was within range of the great mountain, Yü transformed himself into a giant black bear with mighty claws and powerful shoulders in preparation for the gruelling work ahead. Then, after he had tied the drum to a tree behind him, he stooped to the ground and tossed a boulder high into a crevice of the mountain where he could see it had originally broken loose. One after another he tossed the huge boulders in the same direction until almost all the gaps in the mountain had been filled in and the towering structure took on a more solid appearance again. But just as his work was coming to an end, Yü allowed one of the boulders to slip from his upraised arms and it slid over his shoulder, striking the drum that remained tied to the tree.

At once, Nu Jiao prepared a small parcel of food for her husband and set off in the direction of Huanyan Mountain. Arriving at the place where the drum dangled in the breeze, she looked around for Yü, but was confronted instead by a terrifying black bear. Screaming in fright, Nu Jiao ran as fast as her legs would carry her towards her home, pursued by Yü who failed to realize that he had not changed back into his human shape. The young woman ran onwards in panic and dread, faster and faster, until all colour had drained from her face and her muscles grew stiff from the chase. At last, she dropped down to the earth, exhausted and beaten, and within seconds she was transformed into a stone.

Stunned and horrified by what had happened, Yü called out to his wife: 'Give me my son, my only precious son.' Immediately, the stone burst open and a small baby tumbled on to the earth. Yü named the child Qi, meaning 'cracked stone', and the story of his unusual birth earned him great fame even before he had grown to manhood.

✳　✳　✳

OTHER GODS

he ordinary Chinese people seemed to have had little difficulty amalgamating and absorbing a number of different religious beliefs, resulting in popular superstitions which convey the diverse influences of Confucianism, Taoism and Buddhism. Confucius was a pragmatic man, whose main concern was for the smooth running of the state where individuals took personal responsibility for the creation of a harmonious atmosphere on earth, reflecting that of the Heavens. Taoism argued that there was a natural order in the world determining the behaviour of all things and that even inanimate objects had an existence of their own. Buddhism contributed to society the concept of the transmigration of souls and introduced the notion of an Underworld, presided over by the gatekeeper, Yen Wang.

Overall, Chinese people believed that there was a great deal of communication between heaven and earth. It was widely believed that the Gods lived on earth in the capacity of divine officials, and returned to the heavens regularly to report on the progress of humanity. Even the most humble objects were reputed to possess a guardian spirit, while the elements were considered to be more important Gods, meriting sacrifices and ceremonial worship to keep them in a good temper.

The Kitchen God

THIS IMPORTANT DEITY is said to be a Taoist invention, a God entrusted with the power to punish and reward members of the family under his supervision. In the old days, every Chinese household created a temple for him in a small niche above the kitchen stove where an incense stick burned continuously. From this position, the Kitchen God kept an account of how well the family behaved, compiling his annual report for the attention of the Supreme Being of the Heavens. At New Year, he was destined to return to the firmament to present his report and he was sent on his way with a great deal of ceremony. Firecrackers were lit and a lavish meal prepared to improve his mood. His mouth was smeared with honey, so that only 'sweet' words would escape his lips when he stood before the Supreme Being.

The Door Gods

IT WAS THE IMPORTANT task of these Gods to ward off undesirable visitors and evil spirits from Chinese households and often, pictures of ferocious warriors were pinned on either side of the door for this purpose. These pictures represented two war ministers of outstanding ability from the Tang dynasty who were deified after death to become the Door Gods.

The story unfolds that one day the Emperor fell gravely ill with a high fever and during the night he imagined he heard demons in the passageway attempting to gain entry to his chamber. The Emperor grew increasingly delirious and everyone became concerned for his health. Eventually it was decided that two of his finest warriors, Chin Shu-pao and Hu Ching-te, should stand guard overnight outside his door.

For the first time in many weeks, the Emperor slept soundly and peacefully. Next morning, he thanked his men heartily and from that time onwards his health continued to improve. Soon he felt well enough to release his men from their nocturnal duty, but he ordered them to have their portraits painted, looking as fierce as they possibly could, so that he could paste these on his bedroom door to keep evil spirits away in the future.

The Gods of the Elements

THE NUMBER OF SPIRITS and guardians associated with the elements in Chinese legend is vast. Each of these elements is managed by a Ministry in the Heavens, composed of a large number of celestial officials. Members of these ministries are the most powerful of the guardian spirits, since they control the unpredictable forces on earth, such as fire, thunder, lightning, wind and rain.

Natural disasters caused by these forces occur again and again in Chinese mythology. It is always crucial in these stories to maintain a favourable relationship with the God in charge. The Ministry of Thunder, to take but one example, has a complicated infrastructure. It is presided over by the Ancestor of Thunder, Lei Kung, followed by other officials in order of seniority: Lei Kung, the Duke of Thunder, Tien Mu, the mother of Lightning, Feng Po, the Count of Wind, Yü Shih, the Master of Rain and a string of other lesser Gods.

The Duke of Thunder, Lei Kung, is represented in Chinese legend as an ugly black creature with clawed feet and a monkey's head. In his hand he holds a chisel which he uses to beat on a drum, producing the ferocious noise of thunder. A popular story about him recalls how one day, a youth who had been chopping firewood high in the mountains noticed a thunderstorm approaching and took shelter under a large tree. Suddenly a great fork of lightning struck the tree, trapping the Duke of Thunder underneath its great weight as it fell to the ground.

Opposite: The ancient Chinese firmly believed that Gods lived on earth in the capacity of divine officials regularly reporting back to the Supreme God on mankind's behaviour.

Lei Kung begged the youth to release him, promising to reward him handsomely, until finally the terrified youth agreed to his request. In return for his help, the Duke of Thunder presented him with a book which would teach him to conjure up storms and tempests.

'When you need rain,' the God told him, 'call on one of my four brothers and they will come to your aid. But don't call on me unless it is really necessary because my mood is often unpredictable.'

After he had said this, Lei Kung disappeared and the youth headed back to his village.

Within no time he had become a popular figure among the people who regularly took the opportunity to celebrate his great powers in the local inn. One night, however, the youth became so drunk and disorderly he was arrested and carried off by the police. The following morning, as he was led to court, he called upon the God of Thunder to save him from imprisonment. The God responded immediately and thundered through the air so loudly that the windows of the courthouse were shattered by the noise. Cowering to the floor in terror, the magistrate ordered the youth to be released and dismissed him from the court without imposing any sentence.

From this day onwards, the youth used his power to save many people. For whenever he saw that there was danger of the land becoming dried out, he ordered a great storm to appear overhead and the rains to saturate the soil below.

The Goddess of Mercy

THE MOST POPULAR Goddess of the Buddhist faith is the beautiful Kuan Yin, a deity originally represented as a man, an image completely eclipsed by that of a madonna figure with child in her arms after the mid-seventh century. According to the ancient legend, Kuan Yin was about to enter Heaven when she heard a cry of anguish from the earth beneath her and could not prevent herself from investigating its source. Hence her name translates as 'one who hears the cries of the world'.

Kuan Yin is the patron saint of Tibetan Buddhism, the patron Goddess of mothers, the guardian of the storm-tossed fisherman and the overall protector of mankind. If, in the midst of a fire she is called upon, the fire ceases to burn. If during a battle her name is called, the sword and spear of the enemy prove harmless. If

Opposite:
The Goddess of Mercy is revered all over China and she is considered the overall benefactor of mankind.

prone to evil thoughts, the heart is immediately purified when she is summoned. All over China this Goddess is revered and her image appears not only in temples of worship but in households and other public places.

The Eight Immortals

DURING THE MONGOL OR YÜAN DYNASTY in the thirteenth century, a group of Taoist deities who were known as the 'Eight Immortals', or Pa Hsien, became the new focus of a whole catalogue of Chinese legends, achieving a rapid and widespread popularity. Partly historical and partly mythical figures,[1] the Eight Immortals were said to share a home together in the Eastern Paradise on the isles of Peng-lai. Characters similar to these Gods were celebrated in earlier Taoist tales, but now for the first time they appeared as a group, whose different personalities were intended to represent the whole spectrum of society ranging from young to old, rich to poor, whether male or female in gender. The Chinese were very fond of these characters and their numerous eccentricities, and increasingly they became a favourite subject for artists. They appeared together frequently in paintings, or on pottery and elaborate tapestries, or as statuettes and larger sculptures.

The most famous of the Eight Immortals was known as Li Tiehkuai, a name which means 'Li of the Iron Crutch'. Among the group, he was perhaps the most gifted disciple of Taoism, an immortal reputed to have acquired his great wisdom from the spirit of Lao Tzu himself. After the course of instruction had been completed, it was said that the Great Master summoned Li to the Heavens to assess his ability more closely. Li willingly answered the call and his soul left his body and journeyed upwards towards the firmament.

But before Li departed the earth, he placed one of his own pupils, known as Lang Ling, in charge of his body, ordering him to guard it well for a period of seven days until he returned to reclaim it. After only six days had elapsed, however, the student was called to his mother's deathbed, and because he was reluctant to leave the body exposed to scavengers, he decided to cremate it before he departed.

When Li returned to earth he found only a mound of ashes where his body once lay and his spirit was forced to wander about in search of another host. Fortunately, however, a beggar had just died of

Opposite: The Chinese people were very fond of the Eight Immortals whose different personalities were intended to represent the whole spectrum of society.

1 Please refer to the Glossary for historical dates, where relevant.

starvation in the nearby woods, and Li entered the body without any further delay. But as soon as he had done so, he began to regret his decision, for the deceased beggar had only had one leg, his head was ugly and pointed, and the hair around his face was long and dishevelled. Li wished to leave the vile body he had entered, but Lao Tzu advised him that this would not be wise. So instead, the Great Master of the Heavens sent him a gold band to keep his matted hair in place and an iron crutch to help him move about more easily.

And one of the first benevolent acts Li performed in this human body was to visit the home of his negligent pupil, where he poured the contents of his gourd into the mouth of Lang Ling's dead mother, bringing her back to life instantly. For two hundred years Li roamed the earth in this way, converting people to Taoism and healing them with his medicine. He represents the sick and his emblems are an iron stick and a gourd.

The second of the Eight Immortals was called Han Chung-li, a powerful military figure, who in his younger days rose to become Marshal of the Empire. After Han became converted to Taoism, however, he chose to live the life of a hermit in Yang-chio Mountain. Here, he studied the ways of immortality and stored whatever secrets he discovered in a large jade casket within his cave. Some say that Han Chung-li was highly skilled in the ways of alchemy and that during the great famine he changed base metals, such as copper and pewter, into silver which he then distributed to the poor, saving thousands of lives. A fan of feathers, or the peach of immortality are his emblems, and he is associated with military affairs.

During a visit to Yang-chio Mountain, Lü Tung-pin, the son of a high-ranking government official and a clever young scholar, met with Han Chung-li, who invited him into his cave to share some rice wine with him. Tired from his journey, Lü Tung-pin readily accepted the invitation, but as soon as he tasted the wine he fell into a deep sleep. And while he slept, he had an unpleasant dream which altered the course of his life.

He dreamt that he had married well, fathered several healthy children, and that he had risen to a position of great prominence in his work before his fiftieth year. After this time, he looked forward to a peaceful

retirement, but for some reason, he was exiled in disgrace and his family put to death for his misdemeanours. For the rest of his days, he was condemned to a futile and lonely existence from which he could find no escape. Lü awoke from his dream with a start and began to interpret its meaning. At length, he became convinced of the

vanity of worldly dignities and begged Han Chung-li to accept him as a disciple in order that he might train to be one of the Eight Immortals. He is commonly associated with scholars and is always portrayed carrying a sword.

The fourth Immortal, Chang-kuo Lao, was also a famous hermit who lived in the Heng Chou Mountains. He usually appeared seated on a white donkey which he was able to fold up like a piece of paper and which would resume its former shape once he had sprinkled water on it. Chang-kuo Lao claimed that he was a descendant of Emperor Yao and his special magical powers enabled him to bring fertility to young couples. His emblem is a white mule, or a phoenix feather, and he represents the old.

Tsao Kuo-chiu, who is associated with the nobility and whose emblem is a scribe's tablet, became an Immortal after he renounced the wickedness of his worldly life. Tsao was the eldest of two brothers whose sister was married to the Emperor, Jen Tsung. One day the Empress invited a young graduate and his wife to dine with her at the palace, but disaster struck when the younger brother, Ching-chih, who was notorious for his bad behaviour, allowed himself to become besotted by the lady and decided to murder her husband. After he had committed this crime, the soul of the husband demanded justice from the God Pao and Ching-chih was immediately thrown in prison. Knowing his brother would inevitably face the death penalty, Tsao Kuo-chiu encouraged him to kill the graduate's wife so that no evidence of his crime would remain. But the wife escaped to inform Pao of this second attack and Tsao Kuo-chiu was also thrown in prison to face execution.

Eventually, the Empress intervened on her brothers' behalf and begged the Emperor to grant them both an amnesty. As soon as this happened, Tsao was so grateful he decided to abandon his life of luxury and to live by the doctrines of Taoism. For the remainder of his days Tsao Kuo-chiu lived as a hermit devoting himself to the practice of perfection.

The sixth and seventh Immortals were very young men. Han Hsiang Tzu was the grand-nephew of one of the greatest poets of the Tang Dynasty, and from an early age he was schooled by his uncle in the ways of poetry until eventually his ability far surpassed that of the older man. Shortly afterwards, the youth became a disciple of Lü Tung-pin and at the end of his instruction he was required to climb to the top of the Immortalizing Peach Tree. As he did so, he lost his balance and fell dead to the ground. Miraculously, however, he came to life once more, for he had attained the gift of immortality during the descent. Han Hsiang Tzu is always depicted carrying either a flower-basket or a peach and he represents cultured society.

Lan Tsai-ho, a strolling actor and singer of about sixteen years of age, dressed himself in a tattered blue gown and a black wooden belt, and always wore only one shoe. His life was spent urging people to convert to Taoism and he denounced the material comforts of mortals. When given money, he either strung it on a cord and used it as an instrument to beat time as he sang, or scattered it to the ground for the poor to pick up. His emblem is a lute and he represents the poor.

Only one of the Eight Immortals, Ho Hsien-Ku was a woman and she was always depicted holding a lotus flower or the peach of immortality, presented to her by Lü Tung-pin after she had lost her way through the mountains. While still very young, she chose to live a simple life of celibacy and prayer on Yünmu Ling Mountain. Here, she found a stone known as the Yünmu Shih, 'mother-of-pearl', and was told in a dream to powder the stone and to swallow its dust should she wish to become an Immortal. Ho Hsien-Ku followed this instruction and spent the rest of her days floating around the mountains, picking wild berries which she carried to her mother. Her emblem is a lotus and she represents young, unmarried girls.

❋ ❋ ❋

THE CRANE MAIDEN AND OTHER FABLES

he tales that follow demonstrate the mixture of beliefs and religions that were a part of ancient China. In many of the stories the immortal Gods and human beings interact, not exactly as equals, but not within the rigid hierarchy one might expect; it is perfectly feasible, even customary, for the daughter of a God to marry a human, and for such marriages to be successful. Often, we are also transported into a world of spirits and demons, capable of inhabiting animals with malicious intent. Similarly, humans can become transformed into animals or birds, either as a punishment, through grief, or through the will of the Gods.

The image which we perhaps associate most with Chinese myth is that of the dragon. The Chinese dragon breathes cloud, not fire, and is a creature of awesome beauty. Although quick to anger and terrible in its fury, the dragon was mostly a force for good, representing the male principle, the yang, just as the phoenix represents the female, the yin. Similarly, the monkey represents the irrepressibility of the human spirit, as well as its tendency to mischief and evil.

Most of the tales told here do not have such a formal meaning. Some may try to explain the creation of particular stars, others how various animals came into being; they might be parables illustrating foolishness, or steadfastness, or wisdom. But above all they are for entertainment and enjoyment, telling of a mythical time when Gods and dragons walked the earth, and when human destiny was determined by magic spirits.

How Monkey Became Immortal

MONKEY HAD BEEN BORN from a stone egg on top of the Mountain of Fruit and Flowers, and had received many special powers from the stone. He had led his tribe of monkeys to a safe home behind a waterfall on top of the mountain of his birth, and become their beloved king, ruling wisely for hundreds of years. Their way of life was extremely pleasant, they had all they needed to eat and drink, and were safe from enemies. Yet Monkey was not content.

'However happy we are here,' he told his followers, 'we still have Death to fear. One day Lord Yama of the Underworld will send for us, and we will have to obey. I have heard of Lord Buddha and the other Gods who cannot die, and I intend to find them and learn the secret of immortality.'

Monkey set off for the world of men, and soon learned the whereabouts of a holy man, Master Subhodi, who knew the way to eternal life. Subhodi knew in advance of Monkey's coming, and realizing this was no ordinary animal, accepted him as a pupil, and gave him a new name: Sun, the Enlightened One. Monkey spent twenty years with Master Subhodi, learning of the road to eternal life, and many other skills. He learned to change his shape as he pleased, and to travel thousands of miles in a single leap. And armed with this knowledge he returned to his home.

There he found that a demon had taken control of his tribe, and although he conquered the demon, Monkey realized he needed a proper weapon for the future. He seized upon the iron pillar of the Dragon King of the Eastern Sea. This could be changed at will, from an eight-foot staff for fighting, to a tiny needle that Monkey could carry behind his ear, and he kept it with him at all times.

One day two men came for him with a warrant of death from Lord Yama, and tried to drag his soul to the Underworld. Monkey cried out in vain that he knew the way to eternal life, for the men only tied him more tightly. With a desperate struggle, Monkey freed himself, and taking the needle from behind his ear, turned it into a staff, and knocked the men to the ground. Then, incensed with rage, Monkey charged into the Underworld itself, beating anyone in his way with his cudgel.

Opposite: A great many tales featuring Monkey exist in Chinese legend. He represents the irrepressibility of the human spirit, as well as the tendency towards mischief.

'Bring out the register of the dead,' he demanded. The book was brought to him by the terrified judges, whereupon he found the page with his name on, and the names of all his tribe, and ripped it from the register, tearing it into a thousand pieces. 'Now I am free

from your power,' he cried, and charged back out of the Underworld to his own land. The other monkeys assured him he had been asleep, and must have dreamt all this, but Monkey knew in his heart that it had really happened, and that death held no more sway over them.

Appalled by the trouble Monkey was causing, the Jade Emperor, the most powerful God, offered him high office in Heaven, so that the Gods could secretly keep him under their control. Monkey gladly accepted and was made Master of the Heavenly Stables, but he soon realized this was a derisory post, created only to tame him, and he stormed out of Heaven and returned home. The Jade Emperor sent guards to recapture him, but Monkey defeated them, and the Gods sent to seize him. Eventually the Jade Emperor appeased him by offering him a magnificent palace in Heaven, and a proper position as Superintendent of the Heavenly Peach Garden.

Now Monkey knew that the peaches in this garden, which ripened only once every six thousand years, conferred immortality on anyone who ate them, and so he ignored the order not to touch any of them, and devoured a huge number. Unstoppable now, and furious too that he had not been invited to the great Feast of Peaches, given to the Gods by Wang-Mu, Goddess of the Immortals, Monkey was intent on revenge. So, when the preparations were complete, he put all the servants under a spell, and ate and drank all the food and wine prepared for the guests. Dizzy with drink, Monkey staggered into the deserted palace of Lao Chun, where he stumbled across the five gourds in which were kept the seeds of immortality, and, ever inquisitive, he ate them all. Assured doubly of immortality, Monkey returned home.

The Jade Emperor and all the Gods and Goddesses were furious with monkey, but none could defeat him in battle. Until, that is, the Jade Emperor's nephew, Erlang, aided by Lao Chun and the celestial dog Tien-Kou, managed to chain him, and bring him, securely bound, back to Heaven. Monkey was sentenced to death, and placed in Lao Chun's furnace, in which the seeds of immortality were made. But Monkey was now so powerful that he burst free from the crucible, stronger than ever, and proclaimed himself ruler of the Universe.

Opposite: Monkey and his tribe had an extremely pleasant lifestyle, but still he remained unhappy and was most curious to discover the secret of immortality.

At this, Buddha appeared, and demanded of Monkey what powers he had that entitled him to make such a claim. Monkey replied that he was immortal, invulnerable, that he could change shape at will, and could travel thousands of miles in a single leap. Buddha smiled, and taking Monkey in the palm of his hand, said, 'If you can jump

from out of my hand, I will make you ruler of the Universe and all it contains.'

Monkey laughed at this, and in two mighty leaps found himself opposite the five red pillars that mark the edge of the Universe. Delighted, he wrote his name on one of them as proof that he had been there, and returned to the Buddha.

'I have been to the ends of the Universe in two bounds,' he bragged. 'And now I seek my reward.'

'The ends of the Universe?' asked the Buddha, 'You never left the palm of my hand.' And Buddha showed Monkey his fingers, on one of which was Monkey's name in his own writing. Monkey realized the five pillars were merely the five fingers of the Buddha, and that the whole Universe was contained in his hand, and that he could never be defeated. Afraid for the first time in his life, Monkey tried to run away, but Buddha closed his hand over him, and changing his fingers into the five elements of earth, air, fire, water and wood, created a great mountain in which he imprisoned Monkey.

'There you must stay until you have fully repented and are free of your sins,' Buddha told him. 'At that time someone will come and intercede for you, and then you may be free.' And crushed under the mountains the dejected Monkey was forced to stay.

The Pair of Fools

ONCE, A POOR VILLAGER called Lin unexpectedly found ten pieces of silver, riches beyond anything he had ever owned before. After his first flush of exhilaration at finding such wealth, Lin realized that he must hide the money, as he worked in the fields all day, and it could so easily be stolen from him. He looked despairingly around his sparse, mud-walled hut for a hiding place for the silver, but there was no furniture, no secret cupboards, nothing. Then suddenly he thought of the wall itself, and pausing only to check through the door that no one was coming, he hollowed out a cavity in the mud wall, and poured the silver pieces into it. He quickly covered the hole with fresh mud, and guarded his door against all visitors until the mud had dried and there was no sign of the hiding place.

THE CRANE MAIDEN AND OTHER FABLES

However, the next morning, before he left for the fields, Lin had another attack of nerves. If someone did come into his hut looking for money, there was only one place it could be hidden. There was no furniture, no secret cupboards, only the wall itself. It would be the first place any thief would look. Then Lin had a flash of inspiration, and picking up his brush and ink, he wrote on the wall: 'There are no silver pieces hidden in this wall.' Reassured, he went off to the fields for his day's work.

A few hours later Lin's neighbour, Wan, came to look for him. Seeing no sign of Lin, his eyes were drawn to the writing on the wall, and he chuckled to himself: 'Of course there are no silver pieces hidden in the wall, why should there be?' Then a second thought struck him: Why would Lin say there weren't any, unless there actually were?

Pausing only to check through the door that no one was coming, Wan attacked the wall with vigour and found the ten pieces of silver almost immediately. Delighted, he ran home with them to his own hut, where he was struck by an attack of nerves. What if they searched his hut and found the money, and he was taken before the Judge and tortured until he confessed, and then sentenced to death? He must stop anyone from suspecting his guilt. Suddenly, Wan had a flash of inspiration, and picking up his brush and ink, he wrote on the front of his door: 'I, Wan, an honest man, did not steal the ten silver pieces from the hole in the wall of Lin's hut.'

The Silkworm

MANY CENTURIES AGO a certain man was called up to fight for his Emperor, in the war that was raging on the Chinese borders far, far from his home. The man was distraught at leaving his wife and family, but, being a loyal subject he promptly went away to fulfil his duty. As he left, he instructed the family to look after their farm as best they could, and not to worry unduly as to his fate in the battles that were to come, as all life is in the hands of the Gods.

Try though they might to obey his parting instructions, the family missed him terribly, none more so than his daughter. In her loneliness, the young girl took solace in tending the family's horse, a creature that had been her father's for many years, and one that he loved dearly. Every day she would tenderly groom its fine coat, brush its silky mane, and make sure it had clean hay and enough oats to eat, talking to it all the while about how much she missed her father, and how she prayed nightly for his return. However, what little news reached them from the borders became more and more alarming, and the family began to doubt in their hearts if they would ever see their husband and father again.

One day, the daughter was in the stable tending the old horse and thinking of her father, barely able to hold back her tears in her fear for his safety. 'If only you could gallop from here to the wars and rescue him from his peril,' she murmured. 'If anyone could do that, I swear that I would gladly marry him at once, and serve him joyfully all my days, whatever his state or situation in life.'

Immediately the horse reared up violently, and with a loud whinny, tore at the leash that held him, breaking it in two, although it was made of the strongest leather. With a mighty kick of its powerful front legs, it splintered the stable door and galloped across the courtyard and out of sight before the startled girl could stop it, or even call out to the servants. When it became clear that the horse was not going to return, she made her way sadly to the house to tell of its disappearance, not mentioning the oath she had sworn in front of the animal.

Many days later, the runaway horse reached the Chinese borders, and despite the confusion and destruction caused by the war, managed to find its owner in the camp where he was billeted. The man was astonished to see his old horse, and even more surprised when he could find no message from his family on the animal. Immediately, he feared the worst, and became convinced that some disaster had befallen them, and although he was a brave and true subject, his fears for his family overcame his loyalty. He secretly saddled up the horse, and under cover of darkness he eluded the guards and galloped as fast as possible back to his homeland, and to his farm.

His family were amazed and delighted to find him home again; tears of joy rolled down their cheeks seeing him alive and unharmed by the horrors of war. Only his daughter seemed less than overwhelmed by his

Opposite: The young girl was ashamed to reveal to her father that she agreed to marry the dumb animal who had carried him home from the front lines.

return, and avoided his gaze whenever he looked at her, and answered his questions briefly, without emotion. The man was surprised to find nothing amiss in the household, after all his fears and misgivings, but presumed that the horse had come to fetch him out of devotion, and an understanding that his family missed him so much. In gratitude he

lavished attention on the faithful beast, gave it the best oats and hay and the finest stable, and groomed it himself. The horse, however, refused all food and kindness, and just moped in the corner of its stall, making no sound at all. Only when the daughter of the house came near, which she did as rarely as possible, did the animal seem to come alive; then it would rear up, and whinny and froth at the mouth, so that it took several servants to restrain it.

The father became increasingly worried about the horse, which was becoming distressingly thin. Noticing the effect his daughter had on the beast, he asked her one day if she knew why the animal was behaving in so peculiar a fashion. At first the young girl lied, and said she has no idea of the cause of the problem, but eventually, because she was an honest girl, she told her father of the promise she had made in the stable to marry whomsoever would return her father to her, whatever his state or station in life. The father became extremely angry at her lack of sense and modesty, and confined the girl to her room in the house. He forbade her to so much as peep out of the door if the horse was in the courtyard, so as not to disturb it further; for although the man was very grateful to the horse for its years of service, and its intelligence in finding him in the front lines, he still could not imagine allowing a dumb animal to marry his daughter.

The horse continued to pine and mope, and deprived of even a glimpse of the girl, wasted away more and more, day by day. Eventually the father realized there was only one thing he could do, and sadly he took up his bow and arrow and shot the horse to put it out of its misery. The animal gave a piteous whimper, and died, still looking at the house in which it knew the daughter was imprisoned. The man took off the horse's skin, and placed it in the sun to dry, and then went to tell his daughter what he had been compelled to do. She was thrilled to hear that her problem was solved, and that she would not have to marry a horse, and ran into the courtyard to greet the sun for the first time in days. As she passed the dead creature's hide, it suddenly lifted as if on a gust of wind, and wrapped itself tightly around the girl's shoulders, and then her whole body, and started to spin her round like a top. Whirling faster and faster, the girl cried out, but no one could stop her, and she disappeared out of the farm and into the countryside, carried away on the wind, her cries growing ever fainter.

Appalled, her father ran after the whirlwind his daughter had become, and followed it for many days, although it appeared to get smaller and smaller the further it travelled, until it was barely visible to the naked eye. At last, the whirlwind stopped by a mulberry bush, and breathlessly, the exhausted father rushed up to it. There, on a mulberry bough, he found a small worm feeding on the leaf, and seeing that this was all that was left of his daughter, he took it home, grieving in his heart. He and his wife cared for the worm with tenderness, feeding it thick mulberry leaves every day, and after a week the worm produced a fine thread that glistened and shone, and was soft and cool when woven, and more beautiful to look at than any cloth they had ever seen. They called it silk, and bred more and more of the worms, which became famous throughout the land. And in time silk became one of China's most acclaimed and desired products, and many people profited through its sale, so that in years to come silk weavers throughout the country worshipped thankfully the silkworm girl who had given them such a great treasure through her love for her father.

The Crane Maiden

TIAN KUNLUN was a bachelor, who lived alone with his elderly mother whose one desire in life was to see her son happily married before she died. It was a desire that Tian keenly shared, but they had little money, and he had little chance of finding a suitable bride.

Not far from their home was a beautiful pool of clear, fresh water, shaded by willows, and fringed with rushes. One day, as Tian was on his way to the fields, he heard the sound of girls' laughter coming from the pool, and creeping as silently as he could through the rushes, Tian edged nearer to the water to see whose voice sounded so sweet. Before him he saw three of the most lovely maidens he had ever set eyes on, playing and splashing in the pool, their clothes piled on the bank near him. Entranced, Tian watched for a while, gazing at their beauty, when suddenly he sneezed loudly. Instantly the three young women turned into three white cranes, and beating their fine wings, they flew from the water. Two of them swooped and picked up their clothes and soared away, up and up into the clear sky, but the third was not fast enough, and Tian managed to reach her clothes before her. The bird circled him for a moment, and then returned to the water, again taking on the form of the beautiful maiden Tian had seen first. Bashfully, she begged him to return her clothes, but first he insisted on knowing who she was.

'I am a daughter of the High God, and those were two of my sisters,' the girl answered. 'Our father gave us the clothes to pass between Heaven and earth; without them I cannot return to our home.' Again the girl pleaded with Tian to return them, adding, 'If you do give them back I shall gladly become your wife.'

Tian accepted the offer, thinking what a perfect wife the daughter of the High God would make any man, but he feared that if he returned her clothes, she would simply fly away, and he would never see her again. Instead, he gave her his own coat and leggings, and carried her clothes home with him; the crane maiden unwillingly following behind him.

Tian's mother was thrilled that her son was to marry such a beautiful and high-born girl, and their wedding feast was long and lavish, all their friends and neighbours sharing in their joy. The couple lived together, and learned to love each other, and after a time they had a son, whom they called Tian Zhang, and on whom they both doted.

Some years later, Tian was called away to fight in the wars on the borders of China, many many miles from his home. Before he left, he called his mother to him and showed her his wife's celestial clothes and begged her to keep them well hidden, so that she could never put them on and fly away to Heaven. She promised she would, and found a safe hiding place. Tian then said a tearful farewell to his wife and son, and set off for the wars.

After his departure, the young wife asked her mother-in-law every day for a look at her old clothes, just one quick look.

'If you will let me see them only the once I shall be happy,' she told the old lady. Seeing how desperate the girl was to see them, and fearing for her health if she continued as she was, the woman relented. She fetched the clothes from the bottom of a large chest in her own room, and showed them to her. The crane maiden wept with joy to see them and hugged them to her breast. Then, in a flash, she threw off her human clothes, put on the celestial garments, and, instantly was transformed into a beautiful white crane. Then she flew out the window before the old lady could stop her, up, up into the clear sky.

Opposite: After her husband had left to fight in the wars, the young woman became more determined to try on her old clothes once more.

When Tian returned from the wars, his mother told him the news of the crane maiden's flight, but both knew that there was nothing they could do to bring her back. Tian readily forgave his mother, but his little son was inconsolable, always crying out her name, and looking longingly out of the window, hoping she would return. He wandered the fields looking for her, weeping, and would accept no

comfort from his father or grandmother. One day his cries were heard by a wise old man who sat beneath a willow, and who knew the cause of the boy's grief.

'Go to the pool near your home,' he told the child, 'and you will see three ladies all dressed in white; the one that ignores you will be your mother.'

Tian Zhang did as he was told, and sure enough, there were three girls all in white silk, as the wise man had said. There was the crane maiden, who had so missed her little son, that she had begged her sisters to accompany her back to earth to see that he was happy and well cared for, and to look once more at his face. Tian Zhang boldly walked up to the women, and two of them cried out, 'Sister, here is your child to see you,' but the crane maiden looked away, her eyes wet with tears of guilt and joy intermingled. The boy then knew that this was his mother, and ran to her, and seeing this, the girl broke down and took him in her arms, embracing him as if she would never let him go, weeping, and crying, 'My son, my son.'

After some time, one of the sisters said, 'Sister, it is time for us to go. If you cannot bear to be parted from the child, we will take him back to Heaven with us.'

Between them they lifted the child and flew up, up into the clear sky, all the way to the palace of the High God. He was delighted his daughter was no longer unhappy, and also greatly taken with his grandson, whom he taught personally, telling him of all the things of Heaven and earth. The child was quick to learn, and after a few days the High God gave him eight books, and sent him back to earth with these words: 'Study well, my son, for all knowledge is in these, and you may use them to give great benefit to the earth.'

So Tian Zhang returned to earth, where he found that not a few days, but twenty years had passed on earth, and that he was a young man. He tried to find his earthly family, but his grandmother had died, and his father left for the mountains of the West in grief for having lost mother, wife and child. So Tian Zhang devoted his life to studying the eight books, and armed with the knowledge the High God had given him, he became a renowned scholar and judge. He was granted a high place at the Emperor's court, and was famed throughout the land for his wisdom and his desire to help mankind.

And thousands of miles away, in the mountains of the West, the aged Tian heard of his son's fame, and was content.

The Cuckoo

THERE WAS ONCE A God called Wang, who lived in Heaven, but whose love for the earth and its people was so great that he used to visit it regularly, using his powers to help struggling humanity, and to right wrongs. On one such visit he met a woman, like him an immortal, who had been forced from her original home at the bottom of a deep well, and was now living in the kingdom of Shu, which we would now call Sichuan. The two immortals fell instantly in love with each other, and were soon married; Wang left his home in Heaven and came to live in Shu with his new bride, where they reigned together as king and queen.

Wang and his wife were excellent rulers, kind and caring. Wang taught the farmers how to get the most from their land, which crops would grow best, and how to observe the seasons, so that soon the whole kingdom prospered. Amid all this peace and happiness, only one thing still troubled Wang, the one thing over which he had no power to help his people. Every year the mighty Yangtze river would flood, breaking its banks and destroying vast tracts of farming land, sweeping across all before it, crops, livestock, and people alike. Try as he might, with all the powers of an immortal, Wang could do nothing to control this force of nature, and he bitterly grieved over his impotence.

One day a messenger came to Wang's palace to report a miracle: a corpse had been found floating in the great Yangtze, but floating upstream against the current. Moreover, as soon as the body had been pulled out of the river, it had revived and asked to see the king. Amazed at this report, Wang had the stranger brought before him, and asked him his story. The man said that he came from Chu, several thousand miles downstream from where they now stood, and that he had tripped over a log and fallen into the river. He was unable to explain why he had drifted upstream, but he impressed Wang enormously with his knowledge and understanding of the river and its ways, and he talked of the methods they used in Chu to control the floods, and the damage they could cause. Wang immediately asked the stranger if he could help with their problem, and when the man agreed to try, Wang made him Minister of the River, and accorded him much honour at court.

Not many weeks had passed before the river came into flood again, and the new Minister journeyed far along its banks to try and determine the cause. It did not take him long to find his answer: in the higher country the river ran through a series of ravines too narrow to take the flood waters caused by melting snow on the mountain peaks. This made the river break its banks. He instructed engineers to bore drainage channels through the rock from the main channel, allowing the water to disperse safely, and so preventing flooding further downstream in the valuable farmlands.

Wang was so ashamed that he had not thought of this himself, and so impressed by the stranger's abilities as an engineer, that he decided the stranger would make a better king for his people than himself. Accordingly, he gave over the kingship to the Minister and secretly left the court to go and live in isolation in the mountains of the West. He had been there a very short time, however, when rumours reached him of a disturbing nature. It was said that while the man from Chu had been in the mountains, Wang had seduced his wife, who had come to court only recently, and that the stranger, on his return, had found the two of them together. The rumour told that Wang had handed over the throne in shame and guilt, in return for the man's silence, and had been banished to a life in exile.

So stricken was Wang on hearing this vile and ungrateful gossip, and so regretful of his act of generosity in handing over the throne for the good of his people, that he wasted away in his mountain retreat, and died broken-hearted. The Gods turned his spirit into a cuckoo, whose mournful cry in Chinese calls out 'Better return', reminding people for all time, and especially in the Spring at the time of planting, of Wang's grief at leaving his people, and the land of Shu that he loved.

The Wooden Bridge Inn

THERE WAS ONCE A TRAVELLING merchant called Chao, whose trade took him all over China, and who prided himself on knowing all the roads, and all the inns on those roads, throughout the country. One day, however, finding himself in a strange district with his donkey tiring by the mile, he had to admit his ignorance of the area, so he stopped to ask a farmer where he could find accommodation for the night, and, if possible, purchase a new donkey as he had much further to travel.

The farmer replied that travellers always stayed at the Wooden Bridge Inn, run by a woman called Third Lady.

'And does this Third Lady sell donkeys?' Chao asked the man. 'Oh, yes. Best donkeys in the district,' the man replied. But when Chao asked where these fine animals came from, the man looked uneasy, and would not look Chao in the eye. 'Better ask her that,' he said, 'I have absolutely no idea, I'm afraid.' And without further comment, he returned quickly to his field, and did not look back.

Chao walked his weary animal the mile or so to the Wooden Bridge Inn, which was an inviting and comfortable building, presided over by a young woman who greeted Chao warmly. She introduced herself as Third Lady, and invited him to join the six or seven other guests, who were already drinking cups of wine. Chao stabled his donkey around the back, and joined the others for a delicious dinner of fish, vegetables and rice. While chatting to the other merchants, he admired their capable hostess's ability to make them all welcome, plying her guests with wine until they were quite drunk. Chao, however, was not a drinking man, and left the wine alone, preferring to drink only tea.

As midnight approached, the other guests soon fell into a drunken slumber, and Chao was given a clean and comfortable bed alongside a rush partition, where he lay for a while, musing on his fortune in finding such a pleasant resting place. Just as he was about to drift into sleep, he was startled by a low rumble on the other side of the partition, and fearful that someone might be doing harm to his hostess, he peered through a chink in the rush matting. There was Third Lady, alone, dragging a large trunk across the floor of her room, and Chao watched as she knelt before it, opened the lid, and took out a little wooden man. Intrigued, Chao watched as she next brought out a little wooden ox and a little wooden plough, hitched them together and set the man behind the plough. Then, from a small phial, she sprinkled water over the figures, and to Chao's utter amazement, they began to move, and in no time at all had ploughed up the floor of the room.

Third Lady then gave a tiny seed basket to the little man, who proceeded to sow the field that the floor had become, and immediately green shoots of wheat sprang from the soil, ripened, and were harvested by the tiny farmer, who gave the crop to his mistress. Third Lady quickly ground the corn into flour, and under Chao's astonished gaze, made cakes from it, which she put into the oven to bake. She returned the now lifeless figures to the trunk, and pushed it back to the corner of the room. She then retired for the night, leaving Chao to lie alone in the darkness, wondering at what he had witnessed.

When dawn broke, the guests arose, and Third Lady courteously offered them a breakfast of tea and freshly baked wheat cakes. Chao thanked her profusely, but was determined not to eat his cake, hiding it up his sleeve instead. He then went to fetch his donkey from the stable, ready for the next

Opposite:
Chao's trade took him all over China, and he prided himself on knowing all the roads, and all the inns on those roads in the country.

stage of his journey. As he left the Wooden Bridge Inn, he happened to glance through the door, and he froze in astonishment. The other guests, finishing off their cakes, all suddenly became frenzied, their clothes turning into rough animal hair, their ears growing absurdly long, their voices changing to a grating bray. Within minutes the room

was filled with six or seven donkeys, which Third Lady promptly herded with a stick out of the back of the Inn, towards the stables.

Chao hurried his donkey on its way, grateful to have escaped such a terrible fate; he went on to the capital where his business was, saying not a word to anyone about what he had seen. And when he had concluded his trade, he prepared to return home, stopping off only to buy some wheat cakes identical to the ones Third Lady had made for her guests.

On his return journey, he again stayed at the Wooden Bridge Inn, where the hostess welcomed him warmly. This time Chao was the only guest, and Third Lady cooked him an excellent dinner, and bade him drink the wine freely, which he again declined. At midnight, he retired to the same comfortable bed, and was roused again some time later by the same low, rumbling noise of the trunk being pulled into position. Chao did not even bother to look through the partition, he just allowed himself to drift away into a deep sleep.

The next morning, Third Lady again offered him tea and wheat cakes, but Chao, bringing out those he had bought in the city, said, 'Gracious Lady, please try one of these, they are from the capital, and are said to be particularly fine,' and he handed her the cake of her own making that he had taken a few days before. Third Lady had little option but to thank him, and eat the cake. She took only one bite and immediately her hair grew rough, her ears grew absurdly long, and she turned into a donkey. Chao examined the beast, and was delighted to find it was a strong, powerful beast, infinitely superior to his own decrepit animal, which he promptly set free. Staying only long enough to open the trunk, take out the figures and burn them, so they could do no more harm, Chao then spurred his new mount homewards.

For five years Chao had excellent service from his strange donkey, until one day he was riding through Changan. An old man came up to him, and looking at the donkey, cried 'Third Lady of the Wooden Bridge Inn! I would hardly have recognized you. How you have changed!' Then turning to Chao, he said, 'I congratulate you on preventing her from causing more grief, but she has served her penance now. Please let her go free.' Chao dismounted, and unloaded the beast, which brayed loudly in gratitude. The old man took his sword, and split the creature's stomach in two, and out sprang Third Lady. With a cry of shame, and without looking at Chao or the old man, she ran into the wilderness, and no living person ever saw or heard from her again.

Opposite: Many merchants travelling the land took shelter overnight at the Wooden Bridge Inn, little knowing the fate that awaited them at the hands of Third Lady.

The Three Precious Packets

IN THE FREEZING DEPTHS of a particularly severe winter, a poor student called Niu was travelling to the capital to take his law examinations, so that he could start on the ladder of success that might eventually lead to him becoming a magistrate. As the snow fell, and night darkened around him, Niu stopped at a small inn for some food and shelter. His meagre finances allowed him a bowl of noodles, and some hot rice-wine, and he sat contentedly warming himself in front of the fire.

Suddenly, the door of the inn was thrown open, and in a flurry of snow, an old man staggered into the room. He was dressed in rags, had no shoes on his feet, and was clearly half-frozen, his teeth chattering too much to allow him to speak. Without waiting to be asked, Niu leapt from his seat and offered the man his place in front of the fire, which the wretch took with a grateful nod. Soon he began to recover, but when the landlord asked him what he wanted, he replied, 'I only have money for a bowl of tea, and then I will be off again.' The landlord grunted and went off to get the tea, but Niu, poor though he was, could not bear to think of the man having to face the freezing weather again that night without food. He insisted that the man share his noodles, and when they were rapidly eaten, he ordered more, and then more still, until the stranger had eaten five full bowls. He then stood to go, but Niu insisted he share his bedding and get a good night's rest before facing the winter's anger in the morning. Once again, the man gratefully accepted, and fell asleep almost immediately.

In the morning, Niu settled up with the landlord, using up almost all his money in the process, and was about to leave, when the stranger woke and said, 'Please wait, I have something to give you.' He took Niu outside the inn, and said, 'Although I am in beggar's rags, I am actually a messenger from the Underworld; for your kindness to me last night, when you could ill afford it, I would like to give you these in return,' and from his pocket he took three small, folded packets. 'When you are faced with impossible difficulties, you must burn incense and open one of these; it will help you, but only when your circumstances seem hopeless.' Niu took the packets, and all at once the stranger disappeared on the wind.

Niu continued on his way to the capital, not really believing what the man had said. There he continued his studies and waited for the examinations, but the city was terribly expensive, and he was soon forced to cut down on food to the point where he was close to starvation, his studies suffering badly as a consequence. He was about to return to his village in despair, when he remembered the three packets and, lighting a stick of incense, he opened the first of them. Inside was a slip of paper which read, 'Go and sit outside the Bodhi Temple at noon.' The Bodhi Temple was some miles distant, but Niu went there through the cold, and sat in the freezing snow outside the building, all the while thinking that he must be wasting his time. After a time a monk came out and asked him what he wanted. Niu replied that he just wanted to sit there for a while, and taking pity on this strange man, the monk brought him some tea, and started talking to him. He asked Niu his name, and when Niu told him, the monk reeled backwards in astonishment.

'Are you related to the late Magistrate Niu of Chin-Yang?' he asked, and Niu replied that he was the man's nephew. After asking a few further questions, to assure himself that Niu really was the dead man's relative, the monk said, 'Your uncle was a great benefactor of this temple, but he also left three thousand strings of coins with me for safe keeping. When he died, I was at a loss as to what to do with them, but now that you have miraculously come here, you must take them as his next of kin.'

The astonished Niu was now a very wealthy man, able to live in complete comfort, and concentrate entirely on his studies. However, try as he might, he could not pass the examinations necessary to fulfil his ambition of becoming a Magistrate, and he began to despair. After failing for the third time, Niu was about to give up and return to his village, when he again remembered the three packets, and quickly finding the remaining pair, he lit a stick of incense and opened the second. Inside was a slip of paper which read, 'Go and eat in Shu's restaurant.' Rather baffled, Niu did as he was told. He ordered tea, and sat in the restaurant, wondering what he was doing there. Then, from behind a partition on his right, Niu heard two men in a private room talking, and he could not help overhearing their conversation. 'I am worried,' said one, 'that the questions are too easy. After all, this is an important examination, and we do not want to let standards slip.'

The other replied, 'Tell me the quotations you have set, and I will tell you what I think.' The first man then ran through the list of quotations that were to be set as exam topics, and the astonished Niu realized that he was being told exactly what would be required of him at the next round of examinations. Rushing home, he wrote down all he had heard, and when the time came for the exams he passed with flying colours.

So impressive were his results that he was given an important official post, and very soon became a Magistrate, as he had always wished. He became famous for his fairness and wisdom, and also for his kindness, never turning away any person in need. He always carried with him the last of the three packets, but felt that he would never have to open it, so great was his good fortune. However, when still in middle age, Niu fell ill, and nothing that the doctors or the priests could do seemed able to cure him. At last, with his strength failing, Niu decided to open the last packet. He lit a stick of incense and opened the packet; inside there was a slip of paper which read, 'Make your will.'

Niu knew now that his life was ending. He carefully put all his affairs in order, and said farewell to his family and friends. Then he died, peacefully, and full of contentment at a life well spent, mourned by the whole city, and remembered with love and admiration by the entire population.

The Haunted Pavilion

MANY YEARS AGO a student was walking along a road south of Anyang, heading towards that city. In those days it was common for students to travel the country, seeking knowledge from ancient sites and men of learning throughout China: 'wandering with sword and lute' as it was known.

On this particular night the student arrived at a village some twelve miles short of Anyang, and as night was closing in fast, he asked an old woman if there was an inn nearby. She replied, saying that the nearest inn was some miles distant, whereupon the student remarked that he had just passed a pavilion on the road and that he would rest there. Such pavilions were common in China at that time, used as resting places for weary travellers, and looked after by neighbouring villagers.

Opposite: The town's inhabitants were appalled to discover that the young student wished to spend the night at the haunted pavilion and strongly advised him to go elsewhere.

The old woman went white at the student's words, and told him he must on no account stay in the shelter, as it was cursed with demons, and no one who had stayed there had ever lived to tell the tale. But the student laughed off the dire warning, saying that he thought he could take care of himself, and brushing aside the protestations of the villagers, he set off for the pavilion.

Night fell, but the student did not sleep; instead he lit a lamp and read aloud to himself from one of his books. Time passed; for a long while nothing stirred, until, on the stroke of midnight, the student heard footsteps on the road outside. Peering out of the door, he saw a man in black. The man stopped and called the master of the pavilion.

'Here I am,' came a voice from just behind him, causing the student to jump in surprise. 'What do you want?'

'Who is in the pavilion?' the man in black asked.

'A scholar is in the pavilion, but he is reading his book and not yet asleep,' the voice replied.

At this the man in black sighed, and turned towards the village, and the scholar returned to his reading. Some while later he again heard footsteps, and this time, as he peered of the door, he saw a man in a red hat stop on the road outside the pavilion.

'Master of the Pavilion!' the man cried.

'Here I am,' came the voice from just behind him.

'Who is in the pavilion?' the man in the red hat asked.

'A scholar is in the pavilion, but he is reading his book and not yet asleep,' the voice replied.

At this the man in the red hat sighed too and turned towards the village. Then the student waited for a few minutes, until he was sure there was no one else coming down the road. He crept out of the door, and standing on the road, called out, 'Master of the Pavilion!'

'Here I am,' came the voice from within.

'Who is in the pavilion?' the student asked.

'A scholar is in the pavilion, but he is reading his book and not yet asleep,' the voice replied.

The scholar sighed, and then asked, 'Who was the man in black?'

'That was the black swine of the North,' the voice answered.

'And who was the man in the red hat?'

'That was the Red Cock of the West.'

'And who are you?' the student asked.

'I am the Old Scorpion,' came the reply. At this, the student slipped back into the pavilion, and stayed awake all night, reading his book undisturbed.

The next morning the villagers rushed to the pavilion to see if the student had survived the night, and were astonished to see him sitting on the verandah, strumming his lute. As they gathered round him, bombarding him with questions, the student held up his hand for silence.

'Follow me,' he said, 'and I will remove the curse from this building.' Then he went back inside the pavilion, followed by the villagers. He pulled aside a rotting screen in one corner of the room, and there behind it was a huge black scorpion, many feet long, and ready to strike. With one sweep of his sword, the student split the creature from head to tail, and it fell lifeless to the floor.

Next he asked the villagers where they kept a black pig. 'In the house north of the pavilion,' they answered, and showed him the place. There was a huge black pig, its eyes glinting with demonic fury. Again the student drew his sword, and in moments the pig lay dead at his feet.

'Now, where do you keep a large red rooster?' he asked.

'In a shed to the west of the pavilion,' they answered, and showed him the place. There was an enormous red cockerel, with a huge red comb, and long, sharp talons. With another swish of the student's sword, the bird was decapitated, and lay dead at his feet.

The scholar explained to the startled villagers how he had discovered the identities of the demons, and from that day on, no traveller's rest was ever against disturbed in the pavilion south of Anyang.

The Dragon's Pearl

MANY HUNDREDS OF YEARS AGO a mother and her son lived together by the banks of the Min river in the province of Shu, which we now call Sichuan. They were extremely poor, and the young boy had to look after his mother, who was very old and very ill. Although he worked long hours cutting and selling grass for animal food; he barely made enough to support them both, and was always afraid that ruin lay just around the next corner.

One summer, as the earth grew brown through lack of rain, and the supply of good grass became even more sparse than usual, the young boy was forced to journey farther and farther from home to make any living at all; higher and higher into the mountains he went in search of pasture. Then one day, tired and thirsty, the boy was just about to set out empty-handed on the long homeward journey, when he came across a patch of the most verdant, tall grass he had ever seen, waving in the breeze, and giving off a pleasing scent of Spring. The boy was so delighted that he cut down the whole patch, and joyfully carried it down the mountain to his village. He sold the grass for more than he often earned in a week, and for once he and his sick mother were able to eat a good meal of fish and rice.

The next day the boy returned to the same area, hoping to find a similar patch of grass nearby, but to his complete amazement, the very spot which he had harvested the day before had grown again fully, as green and luscious as before. Once again, he cut down the whole patch and returned home. This happened day after day, and the boy and his mother were delighted by the upturn in their fortunes. The only disadvantage was the distance the boy had to travel every day, a long, hazardous journey into the mountains, and it occurred to him that if this was a magic patch of grass, it should grow equally well in his village as it did in the mountains.

The very next day he made several journeys to the mountains, and dug up the patch, grass, roots, soil and all, and carried it back to a spot just near his house, where he carefully re-laid the plot of earth. As he was doing so, he found to his wonder and delight, hidden in the roots of the grass, the largest, most beautiful pearl he had ever seen. He rushed to show it to his mother, and even with her failing sight, she realized that it must be of enormous value. They decided to keep it safely hidden until the boy could go to the city to sell it in the market there. The old woman hid it at the bottom of their large rice jar, which contained just enough to cover the stone, and the boy went back to re-laying the magic grass patch.

The next day he rushed out of bed to go and harvest his crop, only to find that, far from luxuriant pasture he had expected, the grass on the patch was withered, brown, and obviously dying. The boy wept for his folly in moving the earth and destroying its magic, and went inside to confess his failure to his mother. As he was going into the house, he heard his mother cry out, and rushing to her, found her standing in amazement over the rice jar. It was full to the brim with rice, and on the top of the jar lay the pearl, glinting in the morning sun. Then they knew that this must be a magic pearl. They placed it in their virtually empty money box, and sure enough, the next morning, they discovered that it too was absolutely full, the pearl sitting on top of the golden pile like a jewel on top of a crown.

Opposite: The dragon, an image we associate most with Chinese myth, is often the guardian of water, usually protecting its magic pearl, symbol of its power.

Mother and son used their magic pearl wisely, and became quite wealthy; naturally in a small village this fortune did not go unremarked, and the neighbours who had been kind to the mother and son in their times of hardship now found themselves handsomely repaid, and those in need found ready relief for their distress.

However, the villagers were curious as to the source of this new wealth, and it did not take long for the story of the fabulous pearl to become known. One day the boy found himself surrounded by people demanding to see the stone. Foolishly he took it from its hiding place and showed it to the assembled throng. Some of the crowd grew threatening, jostling and pushing, and asking why the boy should be allowed to keep such a lucky find. The son saw that the situation was about to turn ugly, and without thinking, he put the pearl into his mouth to keep it safe. But in the uproar he accidentally swallowed it with a loud gulp.

Immediately, the boy felt as if he was on fire, his throat and then his stomach was consumed with a heat so intense he did not know how to endure it. He ran to his house and threw the contents of the water bucket down his throat, but it had no impact on the searing pain; he dashed to the well, and pulled up bucket after bucket of water, but to no avail. Although he drank gallon after gallon he was still burning up, and in a frenzy of despair he threw himself down on the banks of the Min and began to lap up the river as fast as he could, until eventually he had drunk it absolutely dry. As the last drop of the mighty river disappeared down his throat, there was a huge crack of thunder, and a violent storm erupted. The earth shook, lightning flashed across the sky, rain lashed down from the heavens, and the terrified villagers all fell to the ground in fear. Still the boy was shaking like a leaf, and his frightened mother grabbed hold of his legs, which suddenly started to grow. Horns sprouted on his forehead, scales appeared in place of his skin, and his eyes grew wider, and seemed to spit fire. Racked by convulsions the boy grew bigger and bigger. The horrified mother saw that he was turning into a dragon before her very eyes, and understood that the pearl must have belonged to the dragon guardian of the river. For every water dragon has a magic pearl which is its most treasured possession.

The river was now filling up with all the rain, and the dragon-boy started to slither towards it, his weeping mother still clinging to his scaly legs. With a powerful jerk, he managed to shake her free, but even as he headed for the torrent, he could still hear her despairing cries. Each time she called out, he turned his huge body to look at her, each writhing motion throwing up mud-banks at the side of the river, until, with a last anguished roar, he slid beneath the waves for the last time and disappeared for ever. And to this day the mud banks on the Min river are called the 'Looking Back at Mother' banks, in memory of the dragon-boy and his magic pearl.

The Dragon King's Daughter

THERE WAS ONCE a student named Liu Yi, who lived in the central region of China, near the great lakes. One day, as he was returning from the capital having successfully taken his examinations, he saw on the road ahead of him a young woman herding a flock of sheep. She was the most beautiful woman Liu had ever seen, but she was deeply distressed, tears coursing down her fair cheeks, her whole body shaking with sobs. Liu's heart went out to the girl, and he got down from his donkey and asked her if there was any way in which he could be of assistance. The girl thanked him through her tears, and explained the cause of her grief.

'My father is the Dragon King of Lake Dongting,' she explained, 'and many months ago he married me to the son of the God of the Jing river, whom I do not love. My husband is cruel to me, and his family torment me, but I cannot complain to my father as Lake Dongting is too far away for me to travel, and the family intercept my messages to him. I know my father would help if he but knew of my grief, but I am so utterly alone and friendless.'

Liu was so touched by the girl's plight that he offered to take the message to her father himself, but he could not see how it could be done.

'Although the shores of Lake Dongting are my home,' he said, 'I am a mere human. How could I ever reach your father's palace in the terrifying depths of the lake?'

The girl replied, 'If you are strong in heart, go to the sacred tangerine tree on the northern shore of the lake. Tie your sash around its trunk, and knock on it three times. From there you will be led to the palace.'

Liu willingly agreed to undertake the journey, and the girl handed him a letter from the folds of her gown. As he remounted his donkey, he called out, 'When you return to Dongting, I sincerely hope that we shall meet again. Then, spurring the animal on, he set off. After a few minutes he looked back, but the girl had disappeared together with her sheep.

Liu went straight to the northern shore of Lake Dongting, and finding the sacred tangerine tree, he tied his sash around its trunk and knocked on it three times as the girl had said. At once the waves of the lake parted, and a man rose up from the depths, and asked Liu what he wanted.

'I must talk to your king,' Liu said. 'It is a matter of the utmost importance.'

The man nodded, and placed a blindfold over Liu's eyes. Liu

became aware of a silence engulfing him, and his body became colder and colder, but he did not flinch. After a time, the blindfold was removed, and Liu found he was in a great palace, beautifully decorated with pearl and other precious stones, and all the warmth flooded back into his body. His guide showed him into a vast chamber, and there, on a mighty throne, sat the Dragon King.

Liu bowed low, and humbly proffered the girl's letter, explaining where and how he had met her on the road from the capital. The Dragon King read the letter, and as he did so great tears rolled down his face, and his huge hands shook. Then he instructed a servant to take the letter to the queen, and said to Liu, 'I thank you for all your trouble. You have taken pity on my daughter, while I did nothing to save her from her suffering. I shall never forget your kindness to her, and your bravery in making this journey.'

At that moment he was interrupted by a loud wailing from the queen's chamber, and the sound of weeping. 'Quickly,' ordered the king with a worried frown, 'tell them to be quiet, or they will arouse Chiantang.'

'Who is Chiantang?' asked Liu, surprised that anything should disturb such a mighty ruler.

The Dragon King explained that Chiantang was his younger brother, once ruler of Lake Chiantang. His quick temper had caused such floods and devastation, even threatening the Five Holy Peaks, that the High God had banished him from the lake, and forgiven him on the understanding that his brother guarantee his good behaviour. 'This news would infuriate him, as he is extremely fond of his niece, and would instantly demand revenge.'

As he spoke, there was a tremendous crash, and the chamber filled with smoke. In a tumult of lightning, thunder and rain, a huge red dragon tore through the hall, clouds streaming from his nostrils, and a mighty roar issuing from his throat. Liu fell to the ground in terror, but the dragon left as quickly as it had appeared.

'That was Chiantang,' the Dragon King explained, helping the terrified Liu to his feet. 'I must apologize for his frightening you like that.' He called for wine and food, and graciously set them before Liu, who soon forgot his fear, as they talked about Liu's career, and life in the capital. A short while later, they were cut short by the arrival of the queen and her train, smiling and laughing amongst themselves. And Liu saw to his amazement that the Dragon King's daughter, whom he had met on the road, was in the group. The king embraced her, and he begged her

Opposite: The Dragon King's Daughter described to Liu her father's kingdom on the shores of Lake Dongting and begged him to make contact with her family.

forgiveness for allowing her to marry such a wretch, and she warmly thanked Liu for his help in rescuing her.

At that moment an elegant, dignified young man walked into the chamber and was introduced to Liu as Chiantang. Once he overcame his initial fear, Liu was delighted to find him a charming individual, courteously thanking Liu for his help, and toasting his health. Chiantang explained to his brother that he had fought the Jing River God and his men, and then visited the High God to explain his actions and apologize if he had done wrong. 'He has generously forgiven me,' he said, 'and I now apologize to you, my brother for my fury in your palace, and to you, honoured guest, for scaring you.'

'I am glad the High God has forgiven you,' said the king. 'And I willingly do so too, but you must be less hasty in future. And now tell me of the battle with the God of the Jing river.'

'It was nothing,' said Chiantang. 'I slew six hundred thousand of his men, and destroyed two hundred square miles of his land, and the battle was as good as won.'

'And what of my daughter's erstwhile husband?'

'I ate him,' replied Chiantang casually, and the conversation was over.

The next day a great feast was held in Liu's honour; the Dragon King lavished gifts on him, and Chiantang drank to his health innumerable times. After much delicious food, and even more wine, Chiantang took Liu aside and said to him, 'The king's daughter has been saved thanks to you. She is a fine woman, aware of how much she owes to you, and as it is clear that you are in love with her, I suggest that you marry her straight away.'

Liu did not know what to say; although he was, as Chiantang had guessed, very much in love with the girl, marriage to the daughter of a God was not to be taken lightly. Nor was the suggestion of a rather drunken dragon to be taken too seriously, especially when Liu considered the possibility of Chiantang's anger at his presumption, if the dragon changed his mind when sober. So, regretfully, Liu talked the tipsy Chiantang out of his idea, and the next day left the palace for his home, laden with gifts, and accompanied by many servants. In his heart, though, he still longed for the Dragon Princess.

Months passed, and the now-wealthy Liu, knowing he could not pine for ever, married a local girl, but she was stricken with fever and soon died. To stave off his loneliness, Liu married again, but his second wife too caught the fever, and soon died. Despairing more and more, Liu married a girl from outside the region, who soon bore him a son. As time went by, Liu began to notice that his wife looked more and more like the Dragon Princess, the lost love of his youth, and after his second son had been born, the woman finally admitted that she was indeed the Dragon King's daughter. She had been bitterly disappointed when Liu turned down her uncle's suggestion, and kept remembering his last words to her on the road from the capital: 'When you return to Dongting, I sincerely hope that we shall meet again.' When Liu's second wife had died, she had seized her opportunity to become the third.

The couple lived together in great happiness, and raised a large family. They frequently visited the Dragon King's palace beneath the deep waters of Lake Dongting, and as Liu became older, they stayed there for longer and longer periods. Eventually they left the land of mortal men entirely, and took up residence with the immortal Dragon King and Queen, and Chiantang, in their immortal home beneath the waves.

The Herdsman and the Weaver Girl

MANY, MANY HUNDREDS of years ago there lived in the palace of the High God in heaven a little weaver girl who spun and wove the most beautiful garments for the Gods, using colours and patterns more gorgeous than anything anyone had ever seen before. The High God was delighted with her efforts, but worried that she worked too hard, and for such long hours every day, and he decided to reward her diligence by giving her a rest from her labours. He determined to send her down to earth to live among mortals for a short time, to allow her to experience new and different pleasures. To ensure that the girl was well cared for, the High God chose for her a husband for her time on earth, a herdsman called Chen-Li, who lived with his two elder brothers on a farm by a great river.

The brothers had divided up the farm on their parents' death, and Chen-Li, being the youngest, had received nothing but an old ox, and the least fertile, most unproductive, piece of land. Here he built himself a rough home, and toiled day and night to make a living from the barren soil; although his life was hard he never complained, nor harboured a grudge against his brothers, for he was an honest youth of stout heart, which is indeed why the High God chose him for the weaver girl.

One evening Chen-Li was sitting watching the sun set over the distant mountains as his old ox munched the grass near by. A feeling of great loneliness came over him, and he said to himself, 'If only I had someone to share my life with, all my hard work would seem worthwhile.' To his complete astonishment, the ox looked up and answered him, saying, 'Do not be so sad, master. I can help you to find a wife who will bring you great joy.' The ox then explained that it was really the Ox Star, sent to earth by the High God as a punishment, to work out its penance in labouring for mankind. It did not mention that it had also been given specific instructions regarding Chen-Li and the weaver girl, but went on to say: 'If you go upstream you will find a beautiful, clear pool, shaded by willows and rushes. There the Heavenly Maidens bathe each afternoon; if you were to steal the clothes of one of them she would be unable to fly back to Heaven, and would have to, according to custom, become your wife.'

Chen-Li did as the ox suggested, and the next afternoon he followed the river upstream, where he found the clear pool, shaded by willows. As he peered through the rushes, he saw the most beautiful girls he had ever set eyes on, laughing and splashing in the crystal waters. Spying their clothes piled on the banks of the pool, he leapt forward and snatched one of the piles; the noise disturbed the girls, who flew from the pool, took up their clothes, and soared away, up into the sky. Only one girl was left, naked in the pool, the little weaver girl, who looked shyly at Chen-Li and said, 'Good Sir, if you would be generous enough to return my clothes, I will gladly come with you and become your wife.' Chen-Li handed her clothes to her without hesitation, so strongly did he believe her promise. Then the girl dressed and, true to her word, followed him home and became his wife.

The couple were extremely happy in their simple existence, so much so that the weaver girl forgot all about the palace of the High God, and her place among the immortals. And in the fullness of time she bore the herdsman a fine son and a beautiful daughter, whom they loved dearly. However, the High God did not forget her, and grew impatient for her return. Eventually, when it became clear that she had no intention of leaving Chenh-Li, he sent down to earth his soldiers to bring her back. The weaver girl was distressed beyond all measure at leaving Chen-Li and her two children, but the soldiers were adamant, and carried her away, up into the sky. Chen-Li looked on in horror, unable to prevent this catastrophe, and he cried out in anguish, 'What can I do? What can I do?'

Opposite:
The weaver-girl was so happy in her earthly home she forgot all about the palace of the High God and her place among the immortals.

CHINESE MYTHS & LEGENDS

The old ox saw his grief, and taking pity on Chen-Li said, 'Master, my earthly form will die soon so that I can return to my celestial home; when I am dead, take off my hide and wrap it around you, and you will be able to follow your beloved.' Saying this, the creature lay down and died at Chen-Li's feet, and, quickly, he did as the ox had instructed him. He picked up his son in one arm and his daughter in the other, and threw the leather hide around him. Instantly, all three soared up into the sky, and began to chase after the weaver girl, who was fast disappearing into the distance.

The High God watched this pursuit with much displeasure, and when he saw that Chen-Li would soon catch up with the weaver girl, he threw down his white silk scarf, which flowed and shimmered like fire between the lovers, forming a great river. Chen-Li called across the fiery torrent to his beloved, but to no avail, since neither could cross it. Defeated, he returned to his desolate home.

When the High God saw how much the weaver girl missed Chen-Li and her children, and how terribly they missed her, his anger abated, and he decreed that once a year, on the seventh day of the seventh month, all the magpies in the world would fly up into Heaven and form a bridge across the fiery river, so that the lovers could cross to each other and meet face to face. Whenever they met, the weaver girl would weep, and her tears fall to earth as drizzling rain; then all the women on earth would sorrow, and say, 'Our sister is weeping again.'

Chen-Li and the little weaver girl spent so much time in the sky, they eventually turned into stars; that is why, when we look up into the night sky, we can still see them both shining there. The fiery river is the Milky Way, on one side is Vega, the bright star that is the weaver girl, and on the other side shines Aquila, with two small stars beside it; which are Chen-Li and his two children. And if you look closely at the Milky Way on the night of the seventh day of the seventh month you will see these two stars meet as the two lovers are reunited for a few, precious hours, giving courage and hope to parted lovers throughout the world.

Opposite: Yu Gong was determined to complete his task of shifting the mountain, every day shovelling the earth even though he appeared to make little progress.

The Foolish Old Man and the Mountains

THERE WAS ONCE a very old man, more than ninety years old, called Yu Gong. He lived with his family in the mountains of the West and their house stood right in front of two great peaks, Taihang and

Wangwu. Every time the old man went anywhere, he had to cross the two peaks, and he hated them with all his soul for always exhausting him.

Eventually he could stand it no longer, and calling his family together, told them that they were going to move the peaks out of the way.

'Where will you put all the earth?' asked his wife, who thought the whole plan insane.

'We'll just carry it all to the shores of the great lake,' replied Yu Gong. And all the men of the family set to work, right down to his youngest nephew.

They carried bucket after bucket, sack after sack of earth and rock away, all the way to the shores of the great lake, but still the mountains seemed no smaller, the climb in the mornings no less strenuous. The wise old man who lived nearby saw all this and laughed at Yu Gong.

'This is madness,' he cried. 'You are old, Yu Gong, your life is like a candle guttering in the wind; stop this nonsense now.'

'Stop now?' replied Yu Gong. 'Don't be absurd. When I die my sons will carry on the work, and their sons after them. The work will continue on down the generations until the great task is finished. You really are no wiser than my youngest nephew.'

And the wise man kept silent, as he had no answer to this.

Now it so happened that a God overheard this exchange, and he went to the High God to warn him of the old man's ambition, fearing the two peaks might one day actually disappear. But the High God was so impressed by Yu Gong's fortitude and determination that he sent two giants

Opposite: The High God sent down two giants to help remove the mountains and Yu Gong never had to climb them again.

to help the old man, and they took the mountains away, one to Yongnan in the South, and the other to Shuodong in the East. And the old man was able to live out his remaining years without ever again having to climb over the twin peaks.

✳   ✳   ✳

GLOSSARY

Buddhism Buddhism arrived in China in the first century BC via the silk trading route from India and Central Asia. Its founder was Guatama Siddhartha (the Buddha), a religious teacher in North India. Buddhist doctrine declared that by destroying the causes of all suffering, mankind could attain perfect enlightenment. The religion encouraged a new respect for all living things and brought with it the idea of reincarnation; i.e. that the soul returns to the earth after death in another form, dictated by the individual's behaviour in his previous life. By the fourth century, Buddhism was the dominant religion in China, retaining its powerful influence over the nation until the mid-ninth century.

Confucius (Kong Fuzi) Regarded as China's greatest sage and ethical teacher, Confucius (551-479 BC) was not especially revered during his lifetime and had a small following of some 3000 people. After the Burning of the Books in 213 BC, interest in his philosophies became widespread. Confucius believed that mankind was essentially good, but argued for a highly structured society, presided over by a strong central government which would set the highest moral standards. The individual's sense of duty and obligation, he argued, would play a vital role in maintaining a well-run state.

Eight Immortals Three of these are reputed to be historical: Han Chung-li, born in Shensi, who rose to become a Marshal of the Empire in 21 BC. Chang-kuo Lao, who lived in the seventh to eighth century AD, and Lü Tung-pin, who was born in AD 755.

Jade It was believed that jade emerged from the mountains as a liquid which then solidified after ten thousand years to become a precious hard stone, green in colour. If the correct herbs were added to it, it could return to its liquid state and when swallowed increase the individual's chances of immortality.

Lao Tzu (Laozi) The ancient Taoist philosopher born in 604 BC, a contemporary of Confucius with whom, it is said, he discussed the tenets of Tao. Lao Tzu was an advocate of simple rural existence and looked to the Yellow Emperor and Shun as models of efficient government. His philosophies were recorded in the *Ta Teh Ching*.

Legends surrounding his birth suggest that he emerged from the left hand side of his mother's body, with white hair and a long white beard, after a confinement lasting eighty years.

Mount Kunlun This mountain features in many Chinese legends as the home of the great emperors on earth. It is written in the *Shanghaijing*, (The Classic of Mountains and Seas) that this towering structure measured no less than 3300 miles in circumference and 4000 miles in height. It acted both as a central pillar to support the heavens, and as a gateway between heaven and earth.

Nü Wa The Goddess Nü Wa, who in some versions of the Creation Myths is the sole creator of mankind, is in other tales associated with the God Fu Xi, also a great benefactor of the human race. Some accounts represent Fu Xi as the brother of Nü Wa, but others describe the pair as lovers who lie together to create the very first human beings. Fu Xi is also considered to be the first of the Chinese emperors of mythical times who reigned from 2953 to 2838 BC.

Pan Gu Some ancient writers suggest that this God is the offspring of the opposing forces of nature, the yin and the yang. The yin (female) is associated with the cold and darkness of the earth, while the yang (male) is associated with the sun and the warmth of the heavens. 'Pan' means 'shell of an egg' and 'Gu' means 'to secure' or 'to achieve'. Pan Gu came into existence so that he might create order from chaos.

Taoism Taoism came into being roughly the same time as Confucianism, although its tenets were radically different and were largely founded on the philosophies of Lao Tzu. While Confucius argued for a system of state discipline, Taoism strongly favoured self-discipline and looked upon nature as the architect of essential laws. A newer form of Taoism evolved after the Burning of the Books, placing great emphasis on spirit worship and pacification of the Gods.

Further Reading

Christie, Anthony, *Chinese Mythology*, Paul Hamlyn, London, 1968 ● Translated by Kiu, K.L., *100 Ancient Chinese Fables*, The Commercial Press Ltd, Hong Kong, 1985 ● Translated by Liyi, Yang, *100 Chinese Idioms And Their Stories*, The Commercial Press Ltd, Hong Kong, 1987 ● Luxing, Wu, *100 Chinese Gods*, Asiapac Books, Singapore, 1994 ● Mackenzie, Donald A., *China and Japan: Myths and Legends*, Senate Books, London, 1994 ● Translated by Wangdao, Ding, *100 Chinese Myths And Fantasies*, The Commercial Press Ltd, Hong Kong, 1988 ● Wei Tang, *Legends and Tales from History*, China Reconstructs, Beijing, 1984 ● Werner, Edward T.C., *Ancient Tales and Folklore of China*, George G. Harrap & Co. Ltd, London 1922

Illustration Notes

Page 3 *Girl seated on a rustic rock chair, woodcut* (British Library, London). Courtesy of The Bridgeman Art Library. **Page 5** *Chinese Buddhist tanka.* Courtesy of The Charles Walker Collection at Images. **Page 7** *Two Mandarins* from a book of Chinese paintings (Victoria & Albert Museum, London). Courtesy of The Bridgeman Art Library. **Page 9** *The Aura of Buddha* from 'The Light of Asia'. Courtesy of Images Colour Library. **Page 13** *Confucius*, by Chinese Artist. Private Collection. **Page 15** *Mongol Archer on horseback* from seals of the Emperor Ch'ien Lung and others (Victoria & Albert Museum, London). Courtesy of The Bridgeman Art Library. **Page 17** *Nü Kua Shih* by Chinese Artist. Private Collection. **Page 18** *Portrait of a Chinese Man* (Private Collection). Courtesy of The Bridgeman Art Library. **Page 21** *Mountain View* (Victoria & Albert Museum, London). Courtesy of The Bridgeman Art Library. **Page 25** *Portrait of Confucius* (Bibliotheque Nationale, Paris). Courtesy of The Bridgeman Art Library. **Page 27** *Emperor Yangdi strolling in his gardens with his wives* (Bibliotheque Nationale, Paris). Courtesy of The Bridgeman Art Library. **Page 30** *Chinese Peasants collecting rice* (Free Library, Philadelphia). Courtesy of The Bridgeman Art Library. **Page 33** *Chinese Paintings on glass, depicting courtly ladies* (Private Collection). Courtesy of The Bridgeman Art Library. **Page 35** *Chiang Tzu-Ya defeats Wén Chung* by Chinese Artist. Private Collection. **Page 39** *Emperor Kang Shi's Tour of Kiang-Han* by Chaio Ping Chen (British Library, London). Courtesy of The Bridgeman Art Library. **Page 40** *Lao Tzu* by Chinese Artist. Private Collection. **Page 45** *Emperor Ouei Tsong (Song Dynasty)* (Bibliotheque Nationale, Paris). Courtesy of The Bridgeman Art Library. **Page 47** From 'Book of Urizen' by William Blake. Courtesy of Images Colour Library. **Page 51** *The Emperor Quin Shihuangdi burning all Chinese books* (Bibliotheque Nationale, Paris). Courtesy of The Bridgeman Art Library. **Page 55** Detail from *Silk painting of an archery contest* (Victoria & Albert Museum, London). Courtesy of The Bridgeman Art Library. **Page 59** *Embroidered and painted Chinese landscape* (Allans of Duke Street, London). Courtesy of The Bridgeman Art Library **Page 61** Detail from *Silk painting of an archery contest* (Victoria & Albert Museum, London). Courtesy of The Bridgeman Art Library. **Page 65** *Dragon with sacred fire-pearl.* Courtesy of The Charles Walker Collection at Images. **Page 69** *Ho Hisien-ku, one of the females of the Eight Immortals.* Courtesy of The Charles Walker Collection at Images. **Page 73** *Hêng Ô* by Chinese Artist. Private Collection. **Page 74** *Kitchen God* by Chinese Artist. Private Collection. **Page 77** *Pa Hsien, the Eight Immortals* Private Collection. Courtesy of Images Colour Library. **Page 78** *Chanf Kuo-lao, one of the Eight Immortals.* Courtesy of The Charles Walker Collection at Images. **Page 81** *Lan ts'ai-ho, one of the females of the Eight Immortals.* Courtesy of The Charles Walker Collection at Images. **Page 85** *Incidents from the Chinese tale of 'The Journey to the West'.* Courtesy of Images Colour Library. **Page 87** *Birth of the Monkey* by Chinese Artist. Private Collection. **Page 89** *Monkey Tree* by Chinese Artist. Private Collection. **Page 93** *A Chinese girl seated looking out of the window* by Lam Qua (Christie's, London). Courtesy of The Bridgeman Art Library. **Page 97** *Mirror Picture, scene of an interior* (Christie's, London). Courtesy of The Bridgeman Art Library. **Page 103** *View of the Summer Palace, Peking* (Bibliotheque Nationale, Paris). Courtesy of The Bridgeman Art Library. **Page 105** *The Seven Sages of the Bamboo Grove* by Fu Pao-Shih (Private Collection). Courtesy of The Bridgeman Art Library. **Page 109** Detail from *A Landscape* by Li Sixun (British Museum, London). Courtesy of The Bridgeman Art Library. **Page 113** *Dragon-Gods* by Chinese Artist. Private Collection. **Page 117** *Embroidered hanging 'Coming of Age'* (Victoria & Albert Museum, London). Courtesy of The Bridgeman Art Library. **Page 121** *Miao Shan* by Chinese Artist. Private Collection. **Page 123** *Li T'ieh-Kuai, one of The Eight Immortals.* Courtesy of The Charles Walker Collection at Images. **Page 125** *Willows and Distant Mountains* by Ma Juan. Courtesy of Zhang Shul Cheng and The Bridgeman Art Library.

Index